Easy Beading

Fast. Fashionable. Fun.

The best projects from the first year of *BeadStyle* magazine

From the editors of BeadStyle magazine

KALMBACH
BOOKS

Acknowledgements

Linda J. Augsburg, Paulette Biedenbender, Stacy Blint, Mindy Brooks, Naomi Fujimoto, Amy Glander, Anne Nikolai Kloss, Carrie Rohloff, Maureen Schimmel, Candice St. Jacques, Beth Stone, Elizabeth Weber, Lesley Weiss, Wendy Witchner

Printed in People's Republic of China

05 06 07 08 09 10 11 12 13 14   10 9 8 7 6 5 4 3 2 1

Visit our website at
http://kalmbachbooks.com

Secure online ordering available

Publisher's Cataloging-in-Publication
(Prepared by The Donohue Group, Inc.)

Easy beading : best projects from the first year of BeadStyle Magazine / from the editors of BeadStyle Magazine.

   p. : ill. ; cm.
Includes index.
ISBN: 0-87116-217-2

1. Beadwork--Handbooks, manuals, etc. 2. Jewelry making--Handbooks, manuals, etc. I. Title: BeadStyle Magazine.

TT860 .E37 2004
745.594/2

Managing art director: Lisa Bergman
Assistant art director: Kelly Katlaps
Photographers: Jim Forbes, William Zuback
Project editors: Karin Buckingham, Julia Gerlach

Contents

On the Cover
Page 44
Enjoy the calming blues and greens of this nature-inspired necklace.
Photo by William Zuback

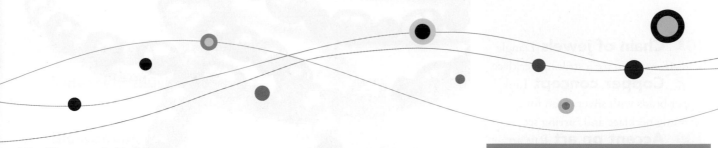

Pearls and shells

Metal and chain

Introduction

Several years ago, not long after I moved to Milwaukee and started beading, I tried to coax one of my neighbors into making jewelry to complement the clothing she sews for herself and for her clients. "Think about it," I urged, knowing her weakness for coordinated accessories. "You could make exactly the right jewelry to go with every one of your outfits."

Naturally, she was skeptical. She'd sewn beads onto fabric as embellishment many times, but had never tried her hand at jewelry. She didn't believe that making jewelry could be as easy as I claimed, but I thought I detected a little bit of interest. I waited patiently for her to get back to me.

A few months later, she told me that she admired a simple knotted necklace in *Bead&Button* magazine, where I was then an associate editor. I introduced her to a local bead shop to gather the necessary supplies, and in no time, she completed two versions of the necklace—one exactly as shown in the instructions, the other with a few of her own variations. It wasn't long before she wanted to know how to attach clasps with crimp beads and how to bend wire into loops.

"You're there," I told her after one evening of instruction. "Now you can make just about anything you'd like."

"That's it?" she asked, eyeing me with considerable doubt. "That's all it takes?"

The answer to my neighbor and to other beginners is, for the most part, yes. Once you can string a few beads, crimp a clasp into place, tie a knot or two, and turn a wire loop, you can make beautiful, fashionable jewelry, the kind of jewelry that fills the pages of *BeadStyle* magazine.

This focus on using a few simple techniques to make wonderful jewelry has been at the core of our concept for *BeadStyle* since our earliest planning meetings at Kalmbach Publishing in 2002. Before the magazine had a name, it had a goal: to publish easy, how-to jewelry articles filled with great ideas, creative bead and color combinations, and endless inspiration. And we wanted this magazine to appeal to experienced beaders as well as beginners.

BeadStyle's first issue went on sale on newsstands in August 2003, and the response was and continues to be extremely positive. Like my neighbor, Lynne Dixon-Speller—now a frequent contributor to *BeadStyle* magazine—people everywhere are discovering the joys of beading. A great sense of accomplishment can be had in the simple act of making something that's greater than the sum of its parts.

The projects in this book are grouped according to the predominant materials used in each piece. You'll find fabulous jewelry in each section—from a vivid red strawberry quartz necklace to a lustrous stick pearl bracelet to a fun and funky jewelry set made from metal washers. Each project has been tested by our editors to ensure that, even if you've never strung beads or used a pair of crimping pliers, you can complete it with confidence. With more than 140 gorgeous earrings, bracelets, necklaces, and more, you're sure to find several you want to make right now.

If you're new to beading, take a moment to look through the following section addressing the tools, materials, and techniques you'll be using throughout the book. The skills are easy to learn and, with a little practice, you'll soon be making your own accessories. In time, you may even become a contributor to *BeadStyle*, like Lynne did. If you're an experienced beader, I'm sure you'll find inspiring designs throughout this book. Whatever your beading experience or skill level, we hope that you'll enjoy this compilation of projects from our extraordinary first year.

Mindy Brooks

Mindy Brooks
Founding editor
BeadStyle magazine

Beading terms

tools and materials

roundnose pliers

chainnose pliers

crimping pliers

split-ring pliers

diagonal wire cutters

bent chainnose pliers

twisted wire needle

flexible beading wire

beading thread /cord

wire

gemstone shapes

twisted oval

faceted button

barrel

cube

teardrop

oval

nugget

slice

chip

faceted teardrop

tube

triangle- or axe-shaped

donut

diamond

round

briolette

pillow-cut

freshwater pearl shapes

rice or oval

potato

teardrop

button

stick

keshi

shell

coin

Basic techniques

Learn the key jewelry-making techniques used in bead-stringing projects in this step-by-step reference

flattened crimp

Hold the crimp bead using the tip of your chainnose pliers. Squeeze the pliers firmly to flatten the crimp. Tug the clasp to make sure the crimp has a solid grip on the wire. If the wire slides, remove the crimp bead and repeat the steps with a new crimp bead.

Make sure the flattened crimp is secure.

overhand knot

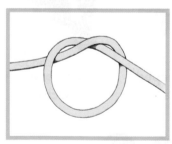

Make a loop and pass the working end through it. Pull the ends to tighten the knot.

folded crimp

Position the crimp bead in the notch closest to the crimping pliers' handle.

Separate the wires and firmly squeeze the crimp.

Move the crimp into the notch at the pliers' tip and hold the crimp as shown. Squeeze the crimp bead, folding it in half at the indentation.

Tug the clasp to make sure the folded crimp is secure.

folded crimp end

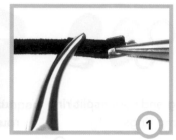

Glue one end of the cord and place it in a crimp end. Use chainnose pliers to fold one side of the crimp end over the cord.

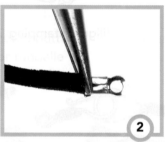

Repeat on the second side and squeeze gently.

surgeon's knot

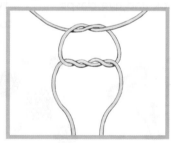

Cross the right end over the left and go through the loop. Go through the loop again. Pull the ends to tighten. Cross the left end over the right end and go through once. Tighten.

plain loop

Trim the wire ⅜ in. (1cm) above the top bead. Make a right angle bend close to the bead.

Grab the wire's tip with roundnose pliers. Roll the wire to form a half circle. Release the wire.

Reposition the pliers in the loop and continue rolling, forming a centered circle above the bead.

The finished loop should have a nice, rounded shape.

10

wrapped loop

Make sure you have at least 1¼ in. (3.2cm) of wire above the bead. With the tip of your chainnose pliers, grasp the wire directly above the bead. Bend the wire (above the pliers) into a right angle.

Using roundnose pliers, position the jaws vertically in the bend.

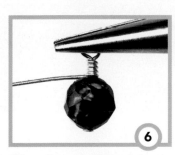

Bring the wire over the top jaw of the roundnose pliers.

Keep the jaws vertical and reposition the pliers' lower jaw snugly into the loop. Curve the wire downward around the bottom of the roundnose pliers. This is the first half of a wrapped loop.

Position the chainnose pliers' jaws across the loop.

Wrap the wire around the wire stem, covering the stem between the loop and the top bead. Trim the excess wire and press the cut end close to the wraps with chainnose pliers.

wrapping above a top-drilled bead

Center a top-drilled bead on a 3-in. (7.6cm) piece of wire. Bend each wire upward to form a squared-off "U" shape.

Cross the wires into an "X" above the bead.

Using chainnose pliers, make a small bend in each wire so the ends form a right angle.

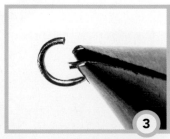

Wrap the horizontal wire around the vertical wire as in a wrapped loop. Trim the excess wire.

split rings

Slide the hooked tip of split-ring pliers between the two overlapping wires.

jump rings

Hold the jump ring with two pairs of chainnose pliers or chainnose and roundnose pliers, as shown.

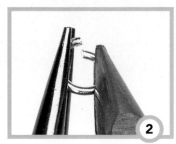

To open the jump ring, bring one pair of pliers toward you and push the other pair away.

String materials on the open jump ring. Reverse the steps to close. ❖

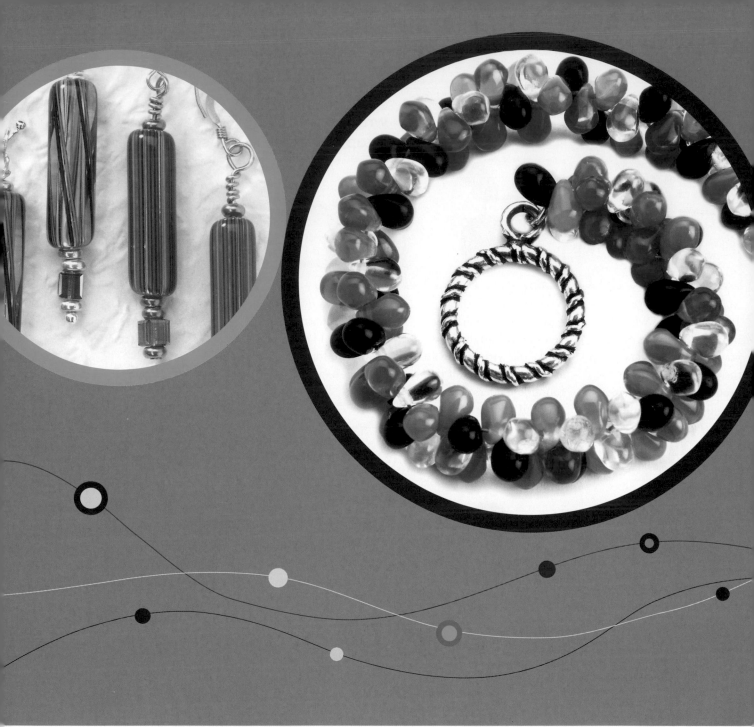

Glass and

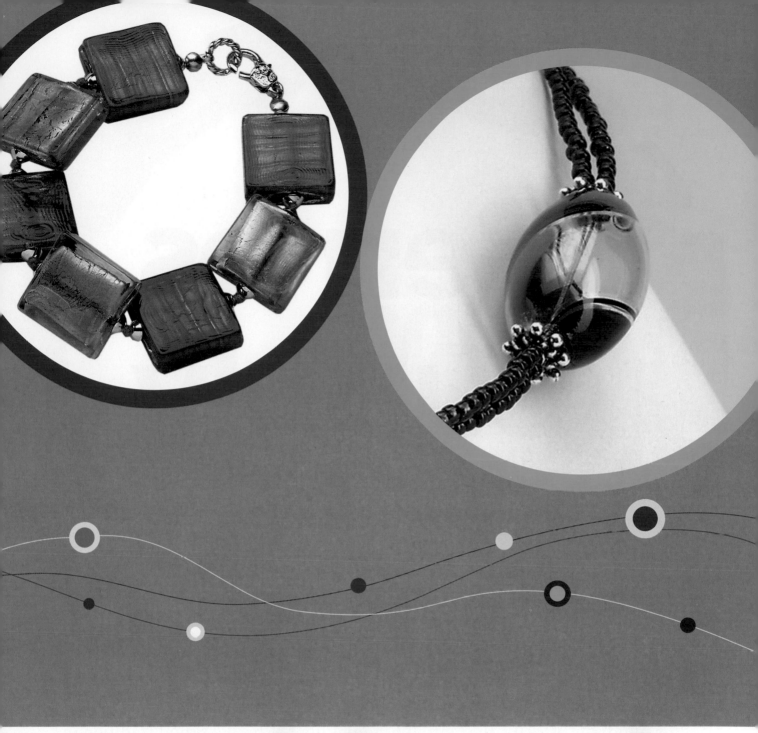

seed beads

Berries and bubbly

by Susan Holland

String a necklace and bracelet of richly colored Venetian beads

For hundreds of years, the craft of beadmaking has been a proud tradition in Venice. In recent years, Venetians have wound molten glass around a copper wire to form individual beads. After allowing the beads to cool, they submerge them in acid to dissolve the wire. The acid method makes silver foil beads susceptible to oxidation, so my husband, Phillip, and I worked with an innovative beadmaker to create beads with white gold.

Six years ago in Murano, I was looking at old glass color charts and found a beautiful persimmon red hue called Rubino Oro. This color would become Rubino Platino when combined with white gold. For this 18-inch necklace, I used a total of 18 beads in Rubino Platino and Champagne Pink.

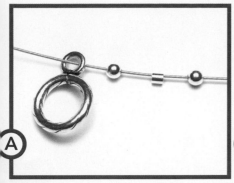

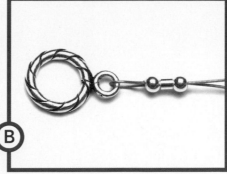

necklace • 1. Cut a 24-in. (61cm) length of beading wire. String a round silver bead, a crimp bead, another round, and the loop end of the toggle clasp. If the hole in your round bead is too narrow for a wire to pass through twice, insert the tip of a roundnose pliers into the hole and twist gently to enlarge it.

2. Go back through these beads and tighten the wire so it forms a small loop around the clasp. Crimp the crimp bead (Basic Techniques, p. 10) and trim the excess wire.

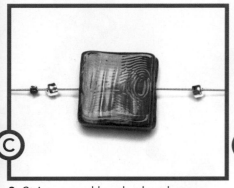

3. String a seed bead, a bead cap, a Venetian bead, and another bead cap. The open end of each bead cap should face the square.

4. Continue stringing this pattern, alternating between raspberry- and champagne-colored squares. Use all 18 squares. End with a bead cap.

5. String a seed bead, a round bead, a crimp bead, another round, and the toggle end of the clasp. Lay the necklace in a circular shape before crimping to make sure it has enough flexibility.

6. Repeat step 2 to finish the clasp.

Supply List

both projects
- flexible beading wire, .018 or .019
- chainnose or crimping pliers
- diagonal wire cutters

necklace
- **9** 20mm square Venetian glass beads, Rubino Platino (all Venetian beads can be found at the Alexander-Lee Gallery, 713-789-2564 or venetianbeads.com)
- **9** 20mm square Venetian glass beads, Champagne Pink
- 5g size 10º or 11º Japanese seed beads, raspberry
- **36** bead caps
- **2** crimp beads
- **4** 3mm round silver beads
- toggle clasp

bracelet
- **4** 20mm square Venetian glass beads, Rubino Platino
- **3** 20mm square Venetian glass beads, Champagne Pink
- seed beads left over from necklace
- **14** bead caps
- **2** crimp beads
- **4** 3mm round silver beads
- toggle clasp

bracelet • Measure your wrist and add 5 in. (13cm) for finishing. Cut a piece of wire to that length. Follow the necklace instructions to string the bracelet and attach the clasp. ❖

1. Determine the finished length of your bracelet, double that measurement, and add 7 in. (18cm). Cut a piece of beading wire to that length and center half the clasp on it.

2. String two drops on each side of the clasp.

3. String a drop on one strand of wire. Pass the remaining strand through the drop in the opposite direction. Tighten the wires, sliding the fifth drop toward the first four, making sure it remains in an upright position.

Do drops

Crisscross drops into a quick and supple bracelet • **by Beth Ruth**

I've always loved teardrop-shaped beads, and felt it was time to showcase them in a project of their own. My decision was to design a watchband but traditional stringing produced a limp and narrow band. A crossweave technique uses more beads, therefore making a more substantial band. Once I refined the process and—realized how quickly the band came together—I opted to make a bracelet. It's so easy, beginners can complete it within an hour.

4. Repeat steps 2 and 3 until your bracelet is ½ in. (1.3cm) shorter than the desired length.

5. String a spacer, a crimp bead, a spacer, and the remaining half of the clasp over both strands. Go back through these beads, tighten the wires, and crimp the crimp bead (Basic Techniques, p. 10). Trim the excess wire. ❖

SupplyList

- **160-180** 4 x 6mm teardrop-shaped beads
- **2** 3mm round spacer beads
- flexible beading wire, .014 or .015
- crimp bead
- toggle clasp
- chainnose or crimping pliers
- diagonal wire cutters

Kits for this bracelet are available at acmebeadcompany.com.

Colorful cubes form a fresh necklace and bracelet

Summer evokes visions of lightweight cotton clothes and picnics on balmy sunny days. I wanted to capture that carefree feeling in a perky and effortless necklace. These cube-shaped beads are not only one of my favorites, but are also available in a smorgasbord of colors. By blending a four-color palette of cubes and a handful of accent beads, an easygoing necklace can be yours in no time. Even if you make only one necklace, the medley of colors in it will spice up your summer wardrobe.

necklace • 1. Determine the finished length of your necklace (mine is 17 in./43cm), add 6 in. (15cm), and cut a piece of beading wire to that length.

String a 2mm round spacer, a crimp bead, a round spacer, and half the toggle clasp. Go back through these beads, tighten the wire, and crimp the crimp bead (Basic Techniques, p. 10).

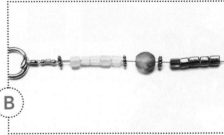

2. String a 5mm flat spacer, five frosted cubes, a spacer, an accent bead, a spacer, and five color-lined cubes. Match the color of the cubes to the preceding accent bead.

Cube-a

C

3. Repeat the pattern shown until you are within ½ in. (1.3cm) of your desired length. End with a flat spacer. Check the fit and add or remove beads as necessary. Finish the necklace as in step 1 with the other half of the toggle clasp.

bracelet • Determine the finished length of your bracelet, add 5 in. (13cm), and cut a piece of beading wire to that length. Follow steps 1 through 3 of the necklace. You may want to use fewer cubes in your bracelet pattern so you can incorporate all the colors used in the necklace. ❖

Supply List

both projects
- flexible beading wire, .014 or .015
- chainnose or crimping pliers
- diagonal wire cutters

necklace
- 4mm frosted cube-shaped beads, 5g each of two colors
- 4mm color-lined cube-shaped beads, 5g each of two colors
- **12** 4-8mm accent beads, **3** each of four colors
- **26** or more 5mm flat spacers

- **4** 2mm round spacers
- **2** crimp beads
- toggle clasp

bracelet
- leftover 4mm frosted cube-shaped beads
- leftover 4mm color-lined cube-shaped beads
- **12** 4-8mm accent beads to match cubes, **3** each of four colors
- **14** or more 5mm flat spacers
- **4** 2mm round spacers
- **2** crimp beads
- toggle clasp

licious

by Anne Nikolai Kloss

3. String the remaining strand of beading wire through the pendant below the first strand. String Delicas to fill the pendant's bail as in step 1. String this strand about ¼ in. (6mm) longer on each end than the upper strand. Tape the ends.

4. Hold the necklace around your neck to check its length. Remove the tape and add or remove beads, if necessary.

Working at one end of the necklace, string two round silver beads, a crimp bead, a round bead, and one section of the clasp on each strand. Go back through the last few beads strung and tighten each wire to form a small loop around the clasp.

5. Repeat step 4 with the remaining pair of wires.

6. Double check the length and add or remove beads as needed. Crimp the crimp beads (Basic Techniques, p. 10) and trim the excess wire.

earrings • 1. Select matching pairs of assorted gemstones, crystals, and spacers. String a head pin with beads as desired. Make the first half of a wrapped loop (Basic Techniques) above the end bead.

2. Complete the wraps and attach the component to an earring wire. Make a second earring to match the first. ✤

Jump!

by Beth Ruth

Needing a new project for a class in my store, I set out to design a quick and easy piece of jewelry. I began maneuvering jump rings and triangle beads, and in less than two hours, I came up with a delightful bracelet that used few components. My customers enjoyed the class so much that they made several more bracelets to give away as gifts.

Connect beaded jump rings to make a shimmering bracelet

1. Using two pairs of pliers, open a jump ring (Basic Techniques, p. 10). Put one bead on the jump ring and close the ring tightly. To close the ring, push the pliers toward each other, go just a hair past, then back to the connecting point. Open another jump ring and add a bead as before. Add this ring to the first jump ring and close it securely.

2. Continue adding beaded jump rings to the chain until you reach the desired length. (My 7½-in./19cm bracelet uses approximately 45 jump rings.) The rings on each end of the bracelet should touch when you wrap the chain around your wrist.

3. To give the bracelet its fullness, begin at one end and add a beaded jump ring to each ring along the chain.

5. At the opposite end, connect six plain jump rings to form a chain. Add six beaded jump rings to the end ring to create an adjustable closure with a jump ring charm. ❖

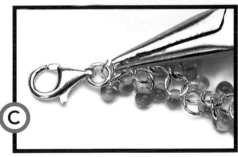

4. Use a jump ring to attach a lobster claw clasp at one end of the bracelet.

Supply List

- **10g** size 5º triangle beads or tiny teardrop beads
- **100-110** 5mm jump rings
- **lobster claw clasp**
- **2 pairs** of chainnose pliers

Kits for this bracelet are available at acmebeadcompany.com.

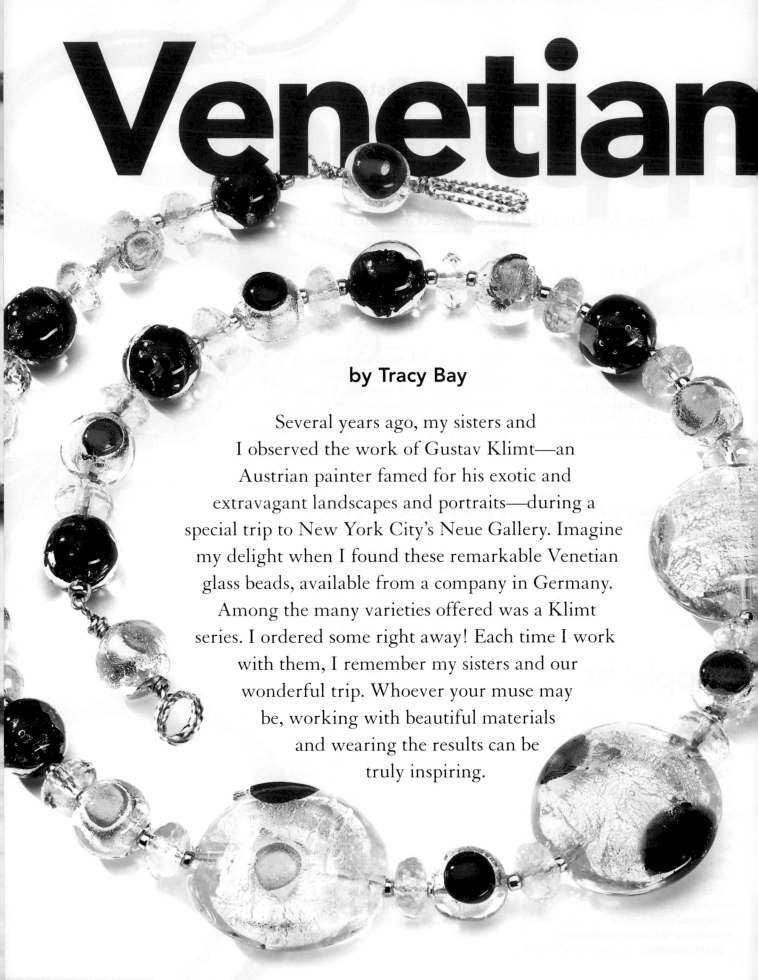

Venetian

by Tracy Bay

Several years ago, my sisters and I observed the work of Gustav Klimt—an Austrian painter famed for his exotic and extravagant landscapes and portraits—during a special trip to New York City's Neue Gallery. Imagine my delight when I found these remarkable Venetian glass beads, available from a company in Germany. Among the many varieties offered was a Klimt series. I ordered some right away! Each time I work with them, I remember my sisters and our wonderful trip. Whoever your muse may be, working with beautiful materials and wearing the results can be truly inspiring.

find

Gilded beads make an inspiring necklace

Klimt (blue) necklace • 1. Determine the finished length of your necklace (mine is 16 in./41cm), add 6 in. (15cm), and cut a piece of beading wire to that length.

2. String a large disc, a spacer, a round bead, and a spacer. Repeat. String a third large disc. Center these beads.

3. On each end, string a spacer, a round bead, a spacer, and a rondelle. Repeat until the necklace is within 1½ in. (3.8cm) of the desired length, considering the clasp length in your measurement.

4. On each end, string a spacer, a round bead, a crimp bead, a rondelle, a spacer, and half the clasp. Go back through the last beads strung and check the fit. Add or remove beads if necessary. If the middle disc does not lie flat, relax the wire a bit. Crimp the crimp beads (Basic Techniques, p. 10) and trim the excess wire.

white necklace • 1. Follow directions for the blue necklace. In step 2, string a large disc, a rondelle, a Mirro round bead, and a rondelle, interspersed with gold beads. Repeat once, then string a disc and a gold bead.

2. In step 3, string a rondelle, a gold bead, a round bead (alternate Mirro and Sommerso round beads in the pattern), and a gold bead. Continue with steps 3 and 4 to complete the necklace. ✤

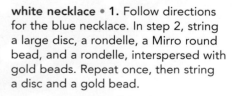

D

6. On one end, string a large-hole bead over the six tails.

E

7. Cut a 4-in. (10cm) piece of wire. Holding the tails with one pair of pliers, use the other pair to wrap the wire snugly around the tails. Don't trim the wire or the tails.

F

8. Slide the leather tails in pairs through a crimp bead and flatten each crimp bead (Basic Techniques) close to the wire-wrapped section.

G

9. Trim the leather tails just beyond the crimps. Bend the wire so it is parallel to the tails.

H

10. String a cone onto the wire, hiding the tails and nestling the large-hole bead in the cone's opening. String a round bead onto the wire, nestling it in the cone's smaller opening.

I

11. Make the first half of a wrapped loop (Basic Techniques) ¼ in. (6mm) above the bead. Slide a soldered jump ring on the loop; complete the wraps.

J

12. Repeat steps 6 through 11 on the other end using the remaining jump ring and the clasp. ❖

Supply List

- **60** 10-12mm glass beads, **20** each of three colors
- 18 ft. (5.5m) 1mm-diameter round leather cord
- **2** 9mm-diameter large-hole spacer beads
- **2** 12 x 11mm plain silver cones (Beaded Wings, beadedwings.com, 405-590-3360)
- 8 in. (20cm) 22-gauge wire
- **6** 3 x 2mm crimp tubes (Beaded Wings)
- **2** 4mm round beads
- S-hook clasp and two soldered jump rings (Beaded Wings)
- chainnose and roundnose pliers
- diagonal wire cutters
- scissors

Double bubble

Loop beads and cord into a fun necklace

by Lynne Dixon-Speller

Rather than display only one blown glass art bead, I chose to double the drama, combine two shapes, and let sheer beauty speak for itself. You may spend more time deciding which beads to use than you will completing this necklace.

SupplyList

- blown glass art bead, approx. 20mm round
- blown glass art bead, approx. 14 x 27mm tube
- 2 ft. (61cm) 2mm-diameter leather cord
- 2 crimp ends
- lobster claw clasp and jump ring
- 6mm split ring
- chainnose pliers
- scissors
- GS Hypo Cement
- split ring pliers (optional)

A

B

C

D

1. Determine the finished length of your necklace, add 3 in. (7.6cm), and cut a piece of leather cord to that length.

Center the round art bead on the cord.

2. Thread each end of the cord through the tube bead in opposite directions. Pull each end to slide the tube bead toward the round bead.

3. Check the fit and trim the leather on each end, if necessary. Glue one end of the cord, place it in a crimp end, and close the crimp end with chainnose pliers (Basic Techniques, p. 10). Repeat on the other end.

4. Open a jump ring (Basic Techniques) and attach it to clasp's loop and end crimp's loop. Close the jump ring. Repeat on the other end of the necklace, substituting a split ring for the jump ring and clasp. ❖

Flash of

A flourish of fringe and a focal bead highlight a double-strand necklace

What's better than escaping winter for the Florida sun? For me, it's taking that vacation with a suitcase of my favorite beads. I love the total relaxation of sipping coffee on the lanai, enjoying the warm breeze, and planning jewelry projects with my beads sparkling in the morning sunlight.

This two-strand fringe necklace took shape as I selected beads to complement a large focal bead. Make yours to suit your taste in length, colors, and number of strands.

Ⓐ

1. Cut two 36-in. (91cm) strands of beading wire. Working forward from the back of the necklace, center three accent beads on both strands.

by **Kim Lucas**

fringe

B

2. Working on one side of the center beads, separate the strands and string a mix of seed beads and accent beads on each strand. After stringing 1½-2 in. (4-5cm) of beads, string an accent bead over both strands. Repeat on the other side of the center beads.

C

3. Continue stringing seed beads and accent beads as in step 2. Work to within 6 in. (15cm) of the end of the wires.

D

E

F

4. Place the wire ends side-by-side. String one accent bead on each pair of wires. Separate the strands and string five to six seed beads on each. String another accent bead and the seed beads as before. String a seed bead and bicone crystal on each pair.

5. String five or six more seed beads on each strand. String a spacer over all four wires.

6. String a furnace bead, a spacer, an accent bead, the focal bead, and a spacer over all four wires.

G

H

SupplyList

- **1** focal bead, approximately 25 x 14mm
- **10g** size 11º seed beads
- **7-10** 4-12mm furnace beads
- **15-20** 3mm bicone crystals
- **50-60** accent beads, assorted shapes, sizes, and colors
- flexible beading wire, .014 or .015
- **4** crimp beads
- **16-26** 4-5mm spacer beads
- chainnose or crimping pliers
- diagonal wire cutters

7. To make the fringe, string each wire with seed beads, accent beads, and spacers. When you are about 2 in. (5cm) from the wire's end, string a crimp bead, one or two seed beads, a small accent bead, and a seed bead.

8. Go back through the accent bead, seed beads, crimp bead, and at least one bead past the crimp. Tighten the wire, but keep the fringe flexible. Crimp the crimp bead (Basic Techniques, p. 10) and trim the excess wire. Repeat to finish the remaining strands. ✤

Tubes and cubes

Furnace glass and crystal make easy earrings

by Karin Buckingham

Gloria Farver's furnace glass bracelet (p. 32) inspired this pair of earrings, but instead of using barrels, wedges, and slices as in the bracelet, I chose long, tube-shaped beads. Cube-shaped crystals and small spacers provide a visual contrast to the strong cylindrical shape of the furnace glass beads.

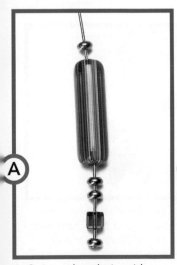

A

1. String a head pin with a spacer, a cube, two spacers, the furnace glass bead, and a spacer.

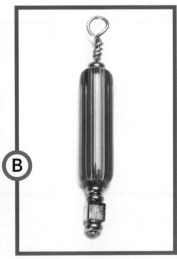

B

2. Make a wrapped loop (Basic Techniques, p. 10) above the end spacer.

C

3. Open the loop on an earring wire and attach the unit. Close the loop.
   Make a second earring to match the first. ❖

SupplyList

- **2** 25mm (approx.) tube-shaped furnace glass beads
- **2** 4mm cube-shaped crystals
- **8** 4mm disc-shaped spacers
- **2** 3-in. (8cm) head pins
- pair of earring wires
- chainnose and roundnose pliers
- diagonal wire cutters

Falling leaves

Combine jump rings and beads for playful earrings

by Linda J. Augsburg

I found these leaf-shaped beads in colors reminiscent of autumn leaves at a local bead shop. Wanting to capture the idea of leaves gently falling to the ground, I decided that linking them together would give the earrings the movement I was seeking. I used a combination of three colors, but the design will work as a monochromatic color scheme as well as in an assortment of colors.

Joining beaded jump rings to linked rings is easier when the linked rings are suspended rather than flat. I slid a paper clip into the last ring and hung it on the hook of a banana holder. (An ornament hanging stand would also work.) This brought the links to eye-level on my desk, making it easier to see what I was doing.

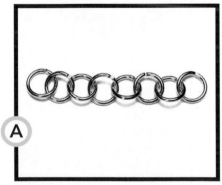

A

1. Link eight jump rings (Basic Techniques, p. 10) to form a chain. Repeat for the second earring.

B

2. Open 36 jump rings. Thread one leaf bead on each. Don't close the jump rings.

C

3. Connect two beaded jump rings to the bottom ring of one chain and close these rings. Work your way toward the top, adding one leaf to each side of each ring in the chain to keep the earring balanced.

Repeat this step on the second chain. You will have four beaded rings remaining. Close these rings.

D

4. Cut the wire in half. Make a small plain loop (Basic Techniques) on one end of each piece. String a dome-shaped bead on each wire and trim the wire to ⅜ in. (1cm) above the bead. Make a second plain loop.

E

5. Open the wire loop on the bottom of the bead unit. Slide on a beaded jump ring, the top link of chain, and another beaded jump ring. Close the loop.

F

6. Open the ring on the earring finding and slide the top loop of the bead unit onto the finding. Finish the second earring to match the first. ❧

Supply List

- **52** or more 5mm jump rings
- Czech glass leaf-shaped beads (I used **18** brown, **10** red, and **8** green)
- **2** 9 x 11mm round- or dome-shaped beads
- pair of earring wires
- 2½ in. (6cm) 20-gauge wire
- roundnose and chainnose pliers
- diagonal wire cutters

Color

As a lifelong beader, I love designing fresh, new pieces. Although the lariat is not a new idea, I gave it my personal spin by alternating contrasting colors of seed beads and showcasing unusual beads in bold color combinations. The lariat incorporates a dangle of larger beads and finishes with a loop closure. Use beads in colors, shapes, and textures that appeal to you; just make sure your ornamental bead is large enough to act as the stopper for the loop closure.

Supply List

- 1 10 x 10mm (or larger) decorative bead
- 12 or more accent beads, assorted sizes and colors
- 10g size 11º Japanese seed beads, 5g each of two colors
- 10 (approx.) spacer beads
- 4 (approx.) bead caps
- 6 (approx.) size 6º seed beads
- 8 (approx.) small rondelles
- flexible beading wire, .014 or .015
- 2 2½-in (6cm) head pins
- 4 crimp beads
- chainnose and roundnose pliers
- diagonal wire cutters

1. To make the end dangle, string assorted spacers and accent beads on a headpin. Cut the head pin ⅜ in. (1cm) above the top bead. Make a loop (Basic Techniques, p. 10).

2. Cut the head off a head pin. Turn a small loop on one end. String an accent bead between two spacers. Cut the head pin ⅜ in. above the end bead and turn another loop.

3. Cut 6 in. (15cm) of beading wire. String the end dangle, a crimp bead, assorted spacers, seed beads, accent beads, and another crimp. Go back through the first crimp and the spacer. Tighten the wire so it forms a small loop around the dangle and crimp the crimp bead (Basic Techniques). Trim the excess wire.

4. String the bead unit from step 2 on the wire's unfinished end. Go back through the crimp and another bead or two. Tighten the wire and crimp the crimp bead. Trim the excess wire.

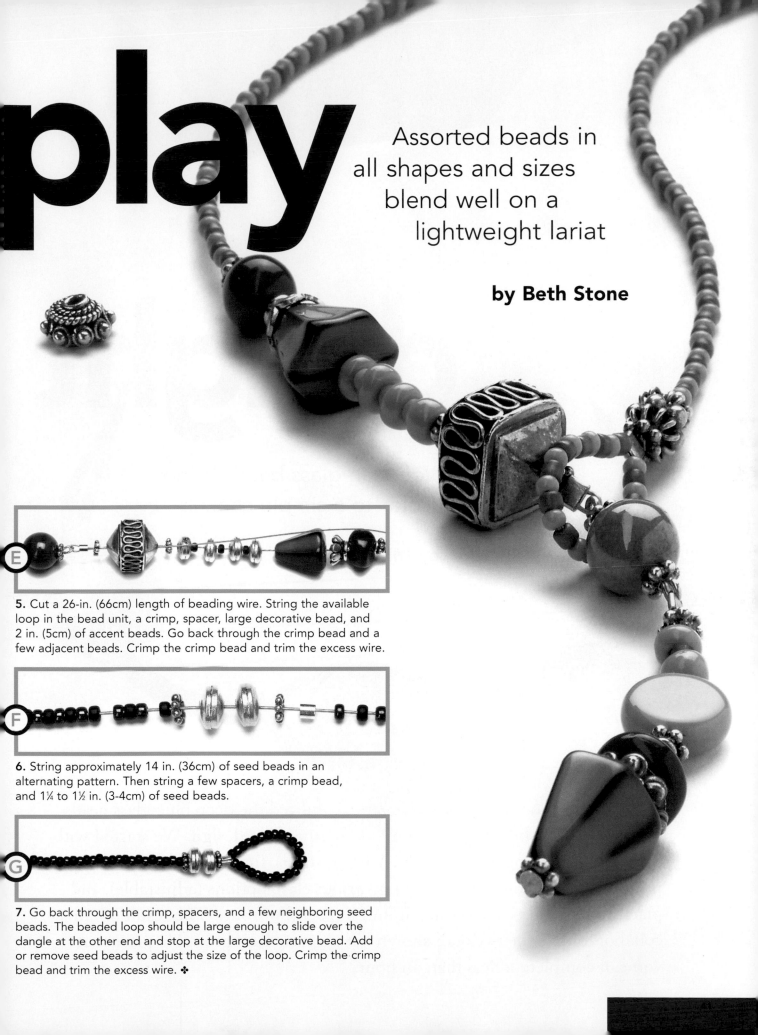

play

Assorted beads in all shapes and sizes blend well on a lightweight lariat

by Beth Stone

E

5. Cut a 26-in. (66cm) length of beading wire. String the available loop in the bead unit, a crimp, spacer, large decorative bead, and 2 in. (5cm) of accent beads. Go back through the crimp bead and a few adjacent beads. Crimp the crimp bead and trim the excess wire.

F

6. String approximately 14 in. (36cm) of seed beads in an alternating pattern. Then string a few spacers, a crimp bead, and 1¼ to 1½ in. (3-4cm) of seed beads.

G

7. Go back through the crimp, spacers, and a few neighboring seed beads. The beaded loop should be large enough to slide over the dangle at the other end and stop at the large decorative bead. Add or remove seed beads to adjust the size of the loop. Crimp the crimp bead and trim the excess wire. ❖

Sheer delight

Translucent Venetian glass beads bring a burst of color to a simple choker

by Mindy Brooks

When one of our company art directors admired the deep blue glass beads on my desk, I asked her to help me come up with a design. We started with the basics: choosing a comfortable length (short), finding a coordinating color palette (monochromatic), weighing various clasp options (adjustable), and placing the focal beads for maximum impact (up front). The result of our collaboration is the necklace shown here, a casual, comfortable piece that you can complete in less than an hour.

A

B

1. Determine the desired length for your necklace and add 6 in. (15cm) for finishing. Cut two pieces of beading wire to that length. Center a spacer, a Venetian bead, and another spacer on both wires.

C

2. Working on either side of the Venetian bead, separate the wires and string an inch (2.5cm) of seed beads onto each one (B). Repeat on the other side (C).

D

E

Supply List

- **3** oval-shaped Venetian glass beads
- 25-30g size 11º seed beads
- **6** flat spacer beads with a 2mm hole
- flexible beading wire, .014 or .015
- 2 in. (5cm) chain
- **4** crimp beads
- lobster claw clasp
- chainnose or crimping pliers
- diagonal wire cutters

3. String a spacer, a Venetian bead, and a spacer onto both wires (D). Repeat on the other side (E).

F

G

H

4. String 5 in. (13cm) of seed beads on each of the four wire ends. Check the length and add or remove beads as needed.

String a crimp bead and a seed bead on each wire on one side of the necklace. Take one of these wires through the clasp and go back through the seed bead, crimp bead, and a few more seed beads. Repeat with the other wire of this pair.

5. Tighten the wires to form small loops around the clasp. Crimp the crimp beads (Basic Techniques, p. 10). Trim the excess wire.

6. String a crimp bead and a seed bead on the unfinished pair of wires. Take each of these wires through the end link of chain and back through the seed bead, crimp bead, and a few more seed beads. Crimp the crimp beads and trim the excess wire. ✤

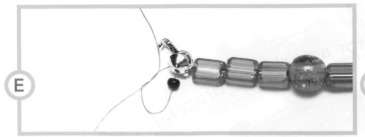

E

F

G

5. Tie a surgeon's knot (Basic Techniques, p. 10) over the bead and tighten the knot so the knot and bead slide into the bead tip. Glue the knot and close the bead tip. When the glue is dry, trim the Fireline close to the bead tip.

For the inner strand, begin with a 34½-in. (88cm) length of Fireline. For the outer strand, begin with a 43½-in. (1.1m) length of Fireline. Repeat steps 1-5 to bead each strand.

6. To make a bead unit, turn a loop at one end of a 2-in. (5cm) piece of wire (Basic Techniques).

7. String a square bead, cut the wire ⅜ in. (1cm) past the bead, and turn another loop. Repeat steps 6 and 7 to make a second unit.

H

I

8. Use one unit to join a three-loop ending connector to the toggle and the other to join a connector to the clasp loop. Open and close the bead unit loops as you would a jump ring (Basic Techniques).

9. Starting with the inner strand, wrap the bead tip's hook around a connector's end loop. Attach the center and outer strands to their respective loops. Repeat to attach the opposite ends, keeping the strands in order.

bracelet • 1. Cut three 19-in. (48cm) lengths of Fireline. Repeat steps 1–5 above, arranging the beads as desired. The clasp adds 1¼ in. (3cm) to the bracelet length.
2. Use a jump ring or split ring to join a lobster claw clasp to the connector. Use a jump ring or split ring to join a soldered jump ring to the connector on the opposite end.
3. Attach the bead tips to the connectors as in step 9.

A

B

Supply List

all projects
- chainnose and roundnose pliers
- diagonal wire cutters

necklace and bracelet
- **1** hank 5mm square silver-lined beads, light blue
- **4** 10mm round beads, lime
- **50** 4 x 7mm faceted button beads, lime AB
- **17** 6mm round beads, lime
- **14** or more assorted cane and lampwork beads
- 4 in. (10cm) gemstone chips or other small beads
- **12** size 11º seed beads

- **12** bead tips
- **4** three-strand ending connectors
- Fireline fishing line, 6 lb. test
- 4 in. (10cm) 20-gauge wire
- **2** 4mm jump or split rings
- **1** 4mm soldered jump ring
- toggle clasp
- lobster claw clasp
- G-S Hypo Cement

earrings
- **6** 6mm round beads, lime
- **2** 10mm round beads, lime
- 16 in. (48cm) 20-gauge wire
- **6** head pins
- **1** pair earring wires

earrings • 1. Make six square bead units as in steps 6 and 7 above. Make two units using a 10mm round bead on each. String six head pins with a 6mm round bead on each. Trim the wire to ⅜ in. (1cm) above the bead and turn a small loop (Basic Techniques).

2. To assemble an earring, join three head pin units to the bottom loop on the 10mm bead unit. Join the 10mm bead unit and three blue bead units as shown. Join the end loop to the loop on the earring wire. Make a second earring to match the first. ❧

Swirls of color

Stringing a six-strand bracelet is easier than you think

by Paulette Biedenbender

Wearing a colorful six-strand bracelet will make everyone take notice. Whether it's composed of beads in the same shape and color or beads in a variety of shapes and a rainbow of colors, you'll want to make one for every occasion.

SupplyList

- **2** 16-in. (41cm) strands 8mm oval fiber optic glass beads
- 10g size 11º Japanese seed beads
- flexible beading wire, .014 or .015
- **6** crimp beads
- three-strand slide clasp
- chainnose or crimping pliers
- diagonal wire cutter

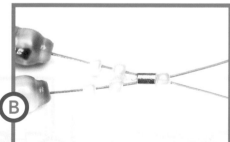

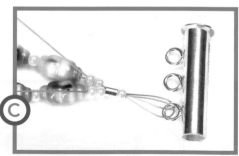

1. Determine the finished length of your bracelet, add 5 in. (13cm), and cut six strands of beading wire to that length. String an alternating pattern of 8mm beads and seed beads on each strand, leaving enough wire for finishing. Begin and end each strand with an 8mm bead.

2. String two seed beads onto the end of each beading wire. String one crimp bead and one seed bead over two wires.

3. String both wires through a clasp loop. Go back through the seed bead and crimp bead. Separate the strands and go through the next two seed beads. Crimp the crimp bead (Basic Techniques, p. 10). Trim the excess wire.
  Repeat steps 2 and 3 to finish the remaining strands. Before attaching the other half of the clasp, be sure to position it opposite the first half. Avoid twisting or crossing the strands. ❖

SupplyList

- **30-35** jasper briolettes, top-drilled
- **25g** size 11º seed beads in five colors (pink, grape, burgundy, cocoa, rust)
- **20g** size 8º seed beads in three colors (pink, fuchsia, rust)
- size 1 Japanese bugle beads, silver
- **10** or more assorted spacers
- flexible beading wire, .018 or .019
- **8** 2mm tube-shaped crimp beads
- **60-80** 1mm crimp beads, with .044 in. hole (Rio Grande, 800-545-6566)
- **2** 7mm soldered jump rings
- **6** 2½-in. (6cm) head pins
- roundnose and chainnose pliers
- diagonal wire cutters
- crimping pliers (optional)

6. String ¾ in. of 8ºs and 11ºs. To finish, string two 8ºs, a crimp bead, spacer, 8º, crimp bead, 8º, and a soldered jump ring. Go back through the last few beads strung, tighten the wire, and crimp the crimp bead. Trim the excess wire.

7. On the reserved beading wire, string two 8ºs, a crimp bead, an 8º, a crimp bead, an 8º, and one of the jump rings. Go back through the beads, tighten the wire, and crimp the crimp beads. Trim the excess wire.

8. String assorted 11ºs interspersed randomly with bugle beads until this strand is approximately 1 in. (2.5cm) shorter than the first strand.

9. String an 8º, a crimp bead, an 8º, a crimp bead, an 8º, and the soldered jump ring at the end of the belt. Go back through the last beads strung. The top strand should be about ½ in. (1.3cm) shorter than the bottom strand. Add or remove beads, if necessary. Crimp the crimp beads and trim the excess wire.

10. To make dangles for the ends, string six head pins with assorted beads and spacers.

11. Make the first half of a wrapped loop (Basic Techniques) above the end beads and connect three dangles to one of the jump rings. Complete the wraps. Attach the remaining dangles to the jump ring at the other end. ❖

Shortcuts

Readers' tips to make your beading life easier

1 fabric inspiration

If you are new to designing bead jewelry and unsure of how to select colors, go to your local fabric store and look at printed fabrics until one catches your eye. Buy a small piece and look at the colors. Then, match beads to the colors and work them into a jewelry design. This approach will work even if you like monochromatic color schemes, because you'll see the range of colors used to achieve that effect. – BETH STONE, VIA E-MAIL

2 enlarging a bead hole

If the hole of a metal bead is too small for multiple strands of wire to pass through, place the bead on the tip of one jaw of your roundnose pliers. Twist the pliers gently a couple times to enlarge the hole. – MAY FRANK, VIA E-MAIL

Editor's note: *We liked this tip so much, we used it in "Berries and Bubbly" (p. 14).*

3 storage options

I like to store beads and stringing materials in electrical tape containers. The containers are small, so they don't take up much space, but they're large enough to store an entire project's components. The lids also double as handy trays while I'm working on a project. – VERONICA STEWART, VIA E-MAIL

4 missing links

If you do a project requiring many beaded links, consider using purchased eye pins. You'll save yourself a lot of work. – YOSHI HARPER, LOS ANGELES, CA

5 unconventional tool

As silly as it sounds, I find that an unbent paper clip works wonders when you need a small, pointed tool. I use the clip to push knots into beads, move errant beads away from a bail, and straighten necklaces on displays. – LISA JEFFERSON, VIA E-MAIL

6 here's the scoop

I make jewelry on a padded board. After I'm done with a project, I use a clamshell to gather any stray beads. It's easy to scoop up beads by pressing the shell lightly into the board, and the shell's curved shape and narrow edge make quick work of pouring tiny beads back into tubes. – LAUREN PROCARIONE, GREENFIELD, WI

7 spooling around

To simplify a stringing project, unroll a length of beading wire slightly longer than what you'll need. Put the plastic spool cover back on and begin stringing. Don't cut the wire until you're ready to add the clasp. Stringing onto the spool reduces the amount of excess wire you use, while keeping the nonworking end of the wire secure.
– GIGI BURGESS, MILWAUKEE, WI

Pearls

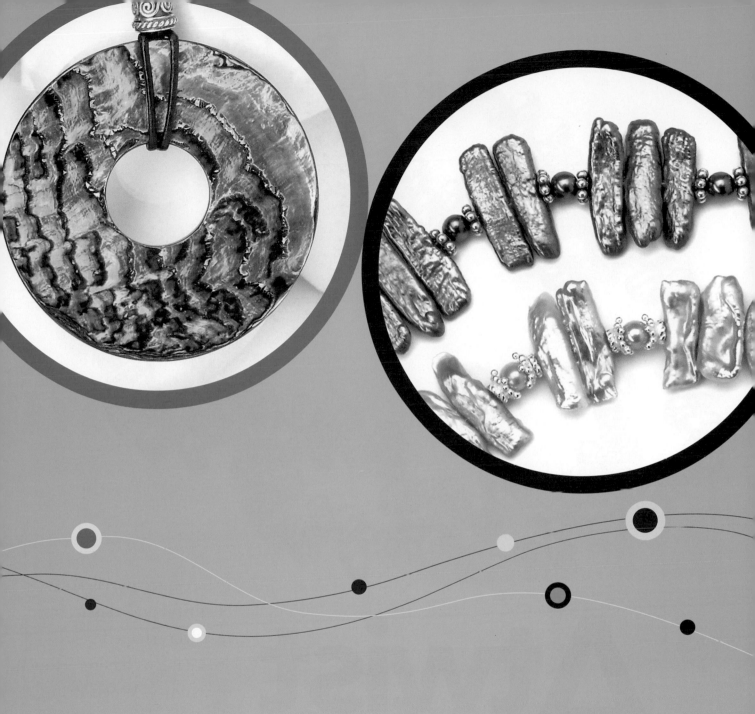

and shells

A twist of pearls

Crystals add sparkle to a
two-strand necklace

by Anne Nikolai Kloss

Freshwater pearls are
beautiful and classic, but
teardrop-shaped pearls
strike me as having a touch
of whimsy. When strung,
these pearls fan out on each
side, giving the finished
necklace an irregular line.
Twisting two strands
together enhances this
effect. For extra sparkle
and shine, string your
necklace with Swarovski
crystals interspersed at
random intervals.

1. Determine the finished length of your necklace (mine is 18 in./46cm), add 6 in. (15cm), and cut two pieces of beading wire to that length. *When stringing a necklace that's meant to be worn with a twist, allow an extra inch or two (2.5-5cm) in length because twisting the strands shortens them.*

String a crimp bead and a 3mm bead and go through one of the clasp's loops. Go back through the beads, tighten the wire to form a small loop around the clasp (photo A), and crimp the crimp bead (Basic Techniques, p. 10). Repeat to attach the second wire to the other clasp loop (photo B).

2. String a 3mm bead on each wire, sliding it over the wire tail. Trim the excess wire. Then string the pearls, adding ten randomly spaced crystals to each strand. Continue until each strand is about ½ in. (1.3cm) short of the finished length.

3. If your clasp is open, close it so you can easily attach the strands without twisting them. Working with the upper strand, string a 3mm bead, a crimp bead, and a 3mm bead and go through the clasp's upper loop. Go back through the last three beads, tighten the wire as before, and check the pearls to make sure no wire shows along the strand. Crimp the crimp bead. Trim the excess wire.

4. Attach the remaining strand to the lower clasp loop, as in step 3. Give the strands a twist when you put on the necklace. ❖

SupplyList

- **2** 16-in. (41cm) strands side-drilled teardrop pearls
- **20** 6-8mm round Swarovski crystals
- flexible beading wire, .014 or .015
- **8** 3mm round beads
- **4** crimp beads
- two-strand clasp
- chainnose or crimping pliers
- diagonal wire cutters

Natural be

Mother-of-pearl pendants shimmer on freshwater pearl necklaces

by Naomi Fujimoto

Centuries ago, some collectors sought the shells of oysters, considering them more valuable than the pearls inside. Mother-of-pearl, the substance secreted by oysters to line their shells, was inlaid in wood, ivory, or bone to create ornate boxes, game boards, picture frames, and tables. I have simpler intentions for the iridescent shell. Its pale champagne shades look beautiful with taupe- or olive-colored pearls, so it serves as a neutral canvas to showcase a delicate gemstone chip or silver finding.

auty

A

round shell pendant • 1. String seven head pins with one teardrop-shaped pearl each. Make the first half of a wrapped loop (Basic Techniques, p. 10) above each pearl. Make the loops 5mm or larger so they'll move freely when they dangle from the pendant.

B

2. Attach each head pin unit to a hole at the bottom of the pendant. Complete the wraps.

C

3. Open a jump ring (Basic Techniques) and pass it through the hole at the top of the pendant. Close the jump ring.

Skip to the instructions for stringing the necklace on the next page.

(A)

oval shell pendant • 1. String a head pin with a gemstone chip or pearl, a flat spacer, and a seed bead. Make a wrapped loop above the end bead.

(B)

2. Open a jump ring and pass it through the hole at the top of the pendant. String the bead unit and a flat spacer, if desired. Close the jump ring.

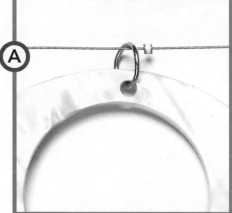

(A)

necklace • 1. Determine the finished length of your necklace (the round pendant necklace is 16 in./41cm; the oval, 15 in./38cm), add 6 in. (15cm), and cut a piece of beading wire to that length. Center a seed bead and the pendant on the wire.

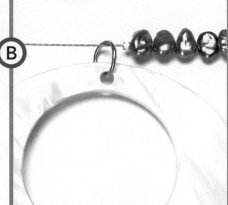

(B)

2. On each side of the pendant, string pearls within 1 in. (2.5cm) of the desired length, interspersing them with seed beads, if you choose.

(C)

3. String a round spacer bead, a crimp bead, a round, and the clasp on one end. On the other end, string a round bead, a crimp bead, a round, and a soldered jump ring. Go back through the last beads strung and tighten the wire. Check the fit and add or remove beads from each end if necessary. Make sure the pendant's jump ring rests on top of the center seed bead. Crimp the crimp beads (Basic Techniques) and trim the excess wire. ❖

Supply List

both necklaces
- flexible beading wire, .014 or .015
- roundnose and chainnose pliers
- diagonal wire cutters
- crimping pliers (optional)

round shell necklace
- round mother-of-pearl pendant, approx. 65mm
- 16-in. (41cm) strand freshwater pearls, approx. 5 x 8mm
- **7** teardrop-shaped pearls, approx. 4 x 6mm
- 1g size 11º seed beads
- **4** 3mm round spacer beads
- **7** 1½-in. (38mm) head pins
- 7mm jump ring
- **2** crimp beads
- lobster claw clasp and soldered jump ring

oval shell necklace
- oval mother-of-pearl pendant, approx. 22 x 28mm
- 16-in. strand teardrop-shaped pearls, approx. 4 x 6mm
- 5mm gemstone chip or pearl
- 1g size 11º seed beads
- **2** flat 3mm spacers
- **4** 3mm round spacer beads
- 1½-in. head pin
- 6mm jump ring
- **2** crimp beads
- lobster claw clasp and soldered jump ring

(mother-of-pearl pendants from Bally Bead Co., 800-543-0280)

String a serene palette of pearls and seed beads

by Beth Stone

Calming effects

Most of us have favorite comfort foods, but a comfort necklace? Like me, you probably have jewelry that you love to wear, pieces that go with everything and make you feel good. If you're looking for that comfort piece, you've come to the right place. This easy necklace will quickly become the one you grab first before you head out the door.

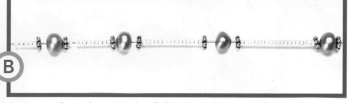

1. Determine the finished length of your necklace (mine is 16½ in./42cm), add 6 in. (15cm), and cut a piece of beading wire to that length.

2. String a stick pearl, five Delicas, a spacer, a 4mm pearl, another spacer, and five Delicas. Repeat this sequence five more times. End with a stick pearl.

3. On each end, string the following sequence: five Delicas, spacer, 4mm pearl, spacer, ten Delicas, spacer, 4mm pearl, spacer, 15 Delicas, spacer, 4mm pearl, spacer, 20 Delicas, spacer, 4mm pearl, spacer. End each strand with 2 in. (5cm) of Delicas.

4. Check the fit and add or remove beads from each end, as needed. On one end, string a spacer, a crimp bead, a 3mm round bead, and the clasp. Go back through these beads, tighten the wire, and crimp the crimp bead (Basic Techniques, p. 10). Repeat on the other end, substituting a jump ring or split ring in place of the clasp. Trim the excess wire. ✤

SupplyList

- **7** freshwater stick pearls
- **14** 4mm button-shaped or round freshwater pearls
- **30** 4mm flat spacers
- **5g** size 15º Delicas
- **2** 3mm round beads
- flexible beading wire, .014 or .015
- **2** crimp beads
- lobster claw clasp
- 5mm soldered jump ring or split ring
- chainnose or crimping pliers
- diagonal wire cutters

by Rupa Balachandar

Beachy keen

String a summery necklace of
freeform mother-of-pearl beads

Summer is all about casual confidence and showing
some skin. Perfect against a summer tan, these
organic mother-of-pearl shards need only a few
accent beads to form a captivating collar. Earrings in
an earthy hue are equally uncomplicated. Possessing
both style and substance, these pieces will take you
from the beach to the bistro—effortlessly.

A

necklace • 1. Determine the finished length of your necklace (mine is 19 in./48cm), add 6 in. (15cm), and cut a piece of beading wire to that length. Center a spacer, round bead, bead cap, focal bead, bead cap, round, and spacer on the wire.

B

2. On each end, string 2¼ in. (5.7cm) of mother-of-pearl shards, a spacer, round, and spacer. Repeat the pattern two more times on each end.

C

3. On one end, string a crimp bead, a seed bead, and half the clasp. Go back through the beads just strung and tighten the wire. Repeat on the other end with the remaining clasp half. Check the fit and add or remove beads, if necessary. Crimp the crimp beads (Basic Techniques, p. 10) and trim the excess wire.

Supply List

necklace
- 16-in. (41cm) strand mother-of-pearl shards
- **8** 8mm round gemstones, picture jasper
- 10 x 12mm focal bead
- **2** bead caps
- **14** 5mm daisy spacers
- **2** size 11º seed beads
- flexible beading wire, .014 or .015
- **2** crimp beads
- clasp
- chainnose or crimping pliers
- diagonal wire cutters

earrings
- **2** 8mm round gemstones, picture jasper
- **2** 5mm daisy spacers
- **2** 3mm Czech fire-polished crystals
- **2** 1½-in. (3.8cm) head pins
- pair of earring wires
- chainnose and roundnose pliers
- diagonal wire cutters

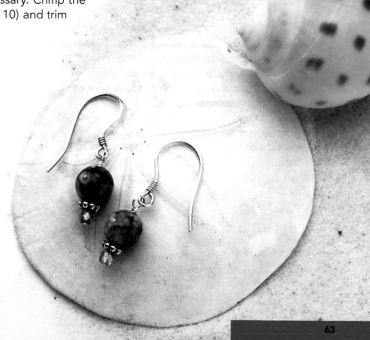

A

B

earrings • 1. String a crystal, a spacer, and a round bead on a head pin. Make a wrapped loop (Basic Techniques) above the bead.

2. Open the loop on an earring wire and attach the dangle. Close the loop. Make a second earring to match the first. ✤

SupplyList

- 45 x 45mm pendant, Hill Tribes silver
- **2** 16-in. (41cm) strands 5-7mm faceted freshwater pearls
- **5** 5mm cube-shaped beads, Hill Tribes silver
- **14** 3mm cube-shaped beads, Hill Tribes silver
- flexible beading wire, .014 or .015
- **4** crimp beads
- **4** 3mm spacer beads
- two-strand clasp
- chainnose or crimping pliers
- diagonal wire cutters

C

3. On the longer wire, center the pendant and string four pearls on each side.

D

4. On each end, string a 3mm cube, a pearl, a 5mm cube, a pearl, and a 3mm cube. String pearls until this strand is 1½ in. longer than the inner strand.

E

5. On both ends of each strand, string a 3mm cube, a crimp bead, and a 3mm spacer bead. String each wire through the corresponding loop of the clasp and back through the beads just strung. Make sure that the clasp is in the correct position. Tighten the wire. Check the fit of both strands, and add or remove an equal number of pearls, if necessary. Crimp the crimp beads (Basic Techniques, p. 10) and trim the excess wire. ❖

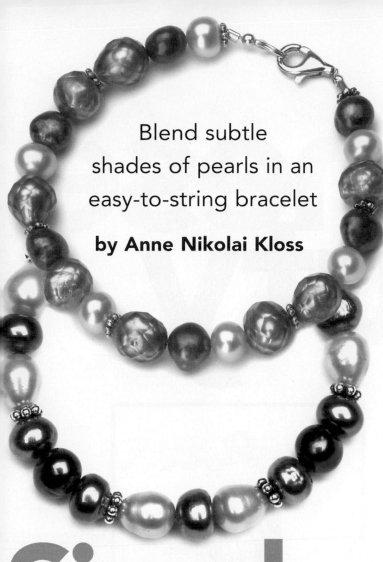

Blend subtle
shades of pearls in an
easy-to-string bracelet

by Anne Nikolai Kloss

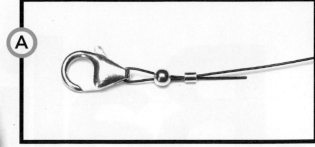

A

1. Measure your wrist, add 5 in. (13cm), and cut a piece of beading wire to that length. String a crimp bead, a round bead, and the clasp. Go back through the round bead and the crimp bead. Tighten the wire to form a small loop around the clasp and crimp the crimp bead (Basic Techniques, p. 10).

B

2. Slide a spacer onto the wire and over the tail. Trim the excess wire. String the pearls interspersed with spacers until the strand fits comfortably around your wrist. End the strand with a spacer bead.

C

3. To finish the bracelet, string a crimp bead, a round bead, and the split ring or soldered jump ring. Go back through the round bead, crimp bead, and spacer. Tighten the wire and crimp the crimp bead. Trim the excess wire. ❖

Simply pearls

Modern cooks often emphasize simplicity, and many wonderful recipes allow the featured ingredient to stand out without much tinkering. I like to take the same approach in making jewelry—sometimes the best designs require the least amount of effort. When you start with a featured ingredient as lovely as freshwater pearls, you don't need to add much to get beautiful results.

Supply List

- **18-25** 8-10mm freshwater pearls, assorted shapes and colors
- **6-10** 3-4mm flat spacer beads
- flexible beading wire, .014 or .015
- **2** crimp beads
- **2** 3mm round beads
- lobster claw clasp
- 5mm split ring or soldered jump ring
- chainnose or crimping pliers
- diagonal wire cutters

Balinese beauty

A

B

necklace • 1. Determine the finished length of your necklace (mine is 18 in./46cm), add 6 in. (15cm), and cut a piece of beading wire to that length. String a few seed beads onto the wire. Center the pendant on the wire, placing it over the seed beads.

2. String 15 quartz rondelles on each side of the pendant.

C

D

3. String a daisy spacer, a bicone, a daisy spacer, and 20 pearls on each end.

4. On each end, string a rondelle, a bicone, a crimp bead, a 3mm round, and half the clasp. Go back through the last beads strung and tighten the wire. Check the fit and add or remove an equal number of beads from each end, if necessary. Crimp the crimp beads (Basic Techniques, p. 10) and trim the excess wire.

Pair soft white pearls with rosy quartz for a feminine look

by Rupa Balachandar

When I begin making a piece of jewelry,
it's like opening a memory book, since I purchase
many of my materials during trips overseas. This
necklace conjures up images of the lush island of
Bali, where I purchased this pretty Osmena
pearl pendant from a silversmith in the village of
Celuk. Although we needed an interpreter to
converse, the artisan and I made a connection.
He made several pieces for me that day, and we
have stayed in touch ever since.

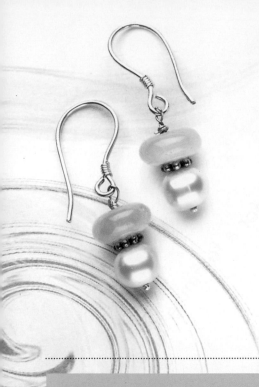

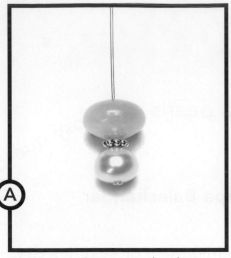

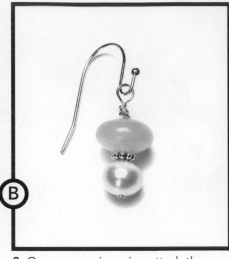

earrings • 1. String a pearl, a daisy spacer, and a rondelle on a head pin. Make a wrapped loop (Basic Techniques) above the top bead.

2. Open an earring wire, attach the unit, and close the earring wire. Make a second earring to match the first.

Supply List

necklace
- mother-of-pearl pendant
- 16-in. (41cm) strand white button pearls, 5-6mm
- 16-in. strand rose quartz rondelles, 10 x 4mm
- **4** 5mm bicone spacers
- **4** 5mm daisy spacers
- **4-6** size 11º seed beads
- flexible beading wire, .014 or .015
- **2** crimp beads
- **2** 3mm round spacer beads
- clasp
- chainnose or crimping pliers
- diagonal wire cutters

earrings
- **2** pearls left over from necklace
- **2** rondelles left over from necklace
- **2** 5mm daisy spacers
- **2** 2-in. (5cm) head pins
- pair of earring wires
- chainnose and roundnose pliers
- diagonal wire cutters

bracelet
- **9** pearls left over from necklace
- **12** rondelles left over from necklace
- **8** flat spacers, 5 x 5 x 3mm square
- flexible beading wire, .014 or .015
- **2** crimp beads
- **4** 3mm round spacers
- clasp
- chainnose or crimping pliers
- diagonal wire cutters

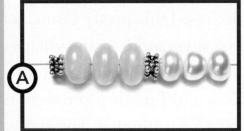

bracelet • 1. Determine the finished length of your bracelet, add 5 in. (13cm), and cut a piece of beading wire to that length. String a spacer, three rondelles, a spacer, and three pearls. Repeat this pattern until the bracelet is the desired length, ending with a spacer.

2. On each end, string a 3mm round, a crimp bead, a round, and half the clasp. Go back through the last beads strung. Check the fit and add or remove an equal number of beads, if necessary. Crimp the crimp beads and trim the excess wire. ❖

Pretty practical

Silver sparkles against leather in this stylish necklace

by Irina Miech

Both contemporary and classic, cultivated and casual, leather necklaces are everywhere. Make your own version with marcasite beads that combine form and function: they lend an Art Deco sparkle and have large holes for stringing. The faceted pearl and neutral colors make this necklace a natural for any outfit—minimal effort for maximum impact.

1. String a pearl on a head pin. Make the first half of a wrapped loop (Basic Techniques, p. 10). Slide the loop into the bail's bottom loop. Complete the wraps.

2. Determine the finished length of your necklace (mine is 18 in./46cm) and cut a piece of leather cord to this length. Center the bail on the leather.

3. On each side of the bail, string a marcasite disc, a large-hole spacer, and a marcasite tube.

4. Check the fit. To shorten the necklace, cut off leather from one of the ends.

Glue one end of the cord and place it in a crimp end. Crimp the crimp end (Basic Techniques). Repeat on the other end.

5. Attach a split ring to the loop in each crimp end. Attach half a toggle clasp to each split ring, or attach a lobster claw clasp to one split ring. ❖

Supply List

- 2 3 x 7mm marcasite disc spacers
- 2 5 x 10mm marcasite tubes
- 2 5 x 7mm large-hole spacers
- faceted pearl, approx. 8 x 11mm
- bail, approx. 6 x 10mm
- 2 ft. (61cm) 1mm-diameter round leather cord
- **2 crimp ends**
- **2 split rings**
- 1½-in. (3.8cm) head pin
- toggle or lobster claw clasp
- E6000 glue
- chainnose and roundnose pliers
- diagonal wire cutters
- split-ring pliers (optional)

Uptown pearls

Crystals and faceted seed beads add sparkle to this easy necklace

by Beth Stone

Partnering modern Bali silver with conventional pearls results in a refreshing rendition of a classic design. Faceted seed beads really catch the light, and combining them with bicone crystals gives an uptown look a little downtown attitude.

SupplyList

- Bali silver focal bead, approx. 10mm
- **2** 8mm rice- or oval-shaped pearls
- **4** 9mm Bali silver bead caps
- **4** 4mm bicone crystals
- **6** 6mm flat spacer beads
- **4** 4mm flat spacer beads (optional)
- flexible beading wire, .014 or .015
- 2g size 11º faceted seed beads, silver
- 2g size 11º faceted seed beads, complementary color
- **2** crimp beads
- toggle clasp
- chainnose or crimping pliers
- diagonal wire cutters

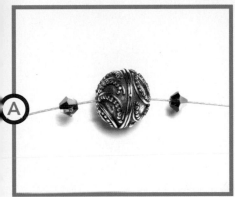

1. Determine the finished length of your necklace, add 6 in. (15 cm), and cut a piece of beading wire to that length. Center the focal bead and two bicone crystals on the wire.

2. String a bead cap, a pearl, a bead cap, a crystal and three 6mm spacers on one end. (If the bead cap holes are large, string a 4mm spacer as shown to prevent the crystals from sliding into the bead caps.) Repeat on the other end of the necklace.

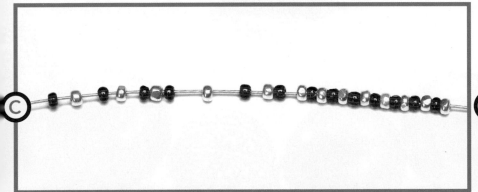

3. On each end, string an alternating pattern of seed beads until the necklace is within 1 in. (2.5cm) of the desired length. Check the fit; add or remove beads as necessary.

4. On one end, string a crimp bead, a seed bead, and half the clasp. Go back through these beads. Tighten the wire, crimp the crimp beads (Basic Techniques, p. 10), and trim the excess wire. Repeat on the other end. ❖

Enjoy the look of fabulous pearls using first-class imitations

Faking it

by Mindy Brooks

Instead of giving in to the temptation of buying expensive South Sea pearls, I found a great-looking, affordable substitute known as shell pearls. These imitations are man-made using shell and other materials, and they come in dramatic sizes, flawless shapes, and believable colors.

Although shell pearls are quite beautiful on their own, they become even more deceptively striking with the addition of a few subtle accent beads in marcasite and silver.

When you're working with imitations, there's one thing to keep in mind: to maintain the high-end illusion, always use the best clasps you can afford.

1. Determine the finished length of your necklace (mine is 17 in./43cm), add 6 in. (15cm), and cut a piece of beading wire to that length.

String a pearl, a crimp bead, a 3mm round, and one clasp section on the wire. Go back through the beads, tighten the wire, and crimp the crimp bead (Basic Techniques, p. 10). Trim the excess wire.

2. String pearls on the beading wire until you reach the desired length. You can enhance the basic pearl necklace by adding a few accent beads along the strand.

3. String a crimp bead, a spacer, and the remaining clasp section. Go back through the last beads strung, including the end pearl. Tighten the wire and crimp the crimp bead. Trim the excess wire. ❖

SupplyList

- 16-in. (41cm) strand 14mm black shell pearls
- assorted marcasite or other accent beads
- flexible beading wire, .018 or .019
- box or safety clasp
- **2** crimp beads
- **2** 3mm round spacer beads
- chainnose or crimping pliers
- diagonal wire cutters

Crystal
clear

A vintage chandelier crystal adorns a pearl necklace
by Naomi Fujimoto

A chandelier crystal makes a striking pendant, particularly when suspended from luminous freshwater pearls. You can purchase crystals from antique stores or flea markets, or turn remnants of an old lamp into fabulous jewelry. Although I prefer the purity of clear and white tones, try a red crystal with garnets for a holiday-worthy presentation. When you wear one of these necklaces, perhaps winter won't seem so cold and gray.

Supply List

- teardrop-shaped crystal, top drilled, approx. 1½ x 2 in. (4 x 5cm) (GSPN Crystals Inc., 800-981-1250 or gspncrystal.com)
- 16-in. (41cm) strand freshwater pearls
- 2g size 10º or 11º seed beads, clear or white
- 4 in. (10cm) 22-gauge silver wire
- flexible beading wire, .014 or .015
- 2 crimp beads
- toggle clasp
- chainnose and roundnose pliers
- diagonal wire cutters
- crimping pliers (optional)

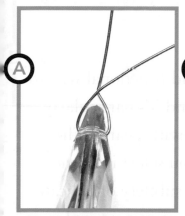

1. Cut a 4-in. (10cm) piece of wire. Slide 1½ in. (4cm) of the wire through the crystal's hole. Bend the wire so it curves up around the top of the bead.

2. Wrap the shorter wire around the longer one as if completing a wrapped loop (Basic Techniques, p. 10). Trim the excess wire close to the wire stem.

3. Make a wrapped loop ⅛ in. (3mm) above the wraps.

4. Determine the finished length of your necklace (mine is 16½ in./42cm), add 6 in. (15cm), and cut a piece of beading wire to that length. Center the pendant on the beading wire.

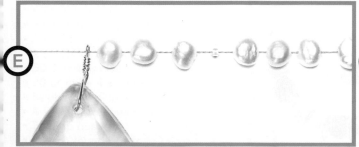

5. On each side of the pendant, string 7¾ in. (20cm) of pearls interspersed with seed beads. Check the fit and add or remove beads as necessary. End with a seed bead.

6. String a crimp bead, seed bead, and one section of the clasp. Go back through the last three beads strung, tighten the wire, and crimp the crimp bead (Basic Techniques). Finish the other end the same way, using the remaining clasp section. ❖

Shell

game

by Monica Lueder

Don't be fooled by this necklace. It's not as difficult as it looks. Leather cord, a paua shell (New Zealand abalone) donut, abalone beads, and sterling silver jump rings are the few elements required to create a simple yet stunning necklace. The bracelet isn't tricky either—a few knots, a few dangles, and you're almost done. Whether you make a necklace, a bracelet, or both, every choice is a winner.

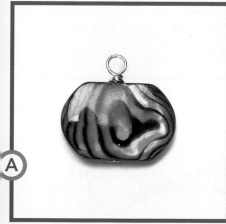

necklace • **1.** String a diamond or oval shell on a 1½-in. (3.8cm) head pin and make a wrapped loop (Basic Techniques, p. 10) above the shell. Make a total of ten wrapped-loop dangles.

2. Cut eight 2-in. (5cm) lengths of 24-gauge wire. (Or snip off the heads of eight 2-in. head pins.) Make a plain loop (Basic Techniques) on one end of each wire. String a diamond or oval shell on six of the wires and make a plain loop above each. String a spacer on each of the two remaining wires and make a plain loop on each end.

3. Fold the leather cord in half. Place the donut on top of the fold and thread both leather strands through the loop to make a lark's head knot around the donut.

D

4. String a barrel-shaped spacer over both strands and make an overhand knot (Basic Techniques) against the spacer.

E

5. On one strand, make an overhand knot ⅜ in. (1cm) away from the center knot. String a large-hole spacer, a wrapped-loop dangle, and a spacer. Make an overhand knot against the spacer.

F

6. Make an overhand knot ⅜ in. away. String a wrapped-loop dangle and make an overhand knot against it. Repeat three times.

7. Repeat steps 5 and 6 on the other strand.

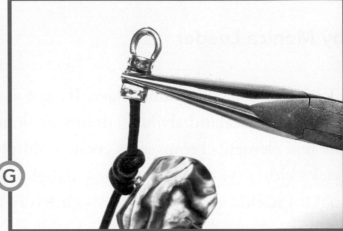

G

8. On each end, cut the cord ⅜ in. away from the last knot. Glue the end and insert it into a crimp end. Flatten the crimp with chainnose pliers. Make sure to flatten only the middle section of the crimp.

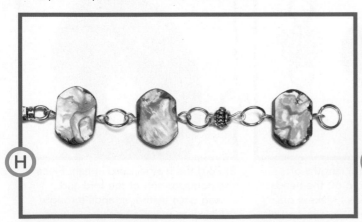

H

9. Open a loop on a shell unit, attach it to the loop on one crimp end, and close the loop. Link the remaining loop to a soldered jump ring in the same manner.

Add a shell unit, soldered jump ring, spacer unit, soldered jump ring, shell unit, and soldered jump ring.

Repeat step 9 on the other end.

I

10. Check the fit. For a longer necklace, make more shell units and attach them with soldered jump rings.

On each end, open a 7mm jump ring. Attach half the clasp and close the jump ring.

A

bracelet • **1.** Make eight shell units, as in step 1 of the necklace. String a crystal on a head pin and make a wrapped loop. Make eight crystal units.

B

2. Open a 6mm jump ring. String a shell unit and a crystal unit and close the ring. Use jump rings to make a total of eight units.

C

3. Make an overhand knot ⅜ in. away from the end of the leather cord. String a spacer, a shell and crystal unit, and a spacer. Make an overhand knot against the spacer. Repeat this sequence seven more times at ⅜-in. intervals.

D

4. Check the fit. If necessary, make additional shell and crystal units and string them as before. Finish each end with a crimp end as in step 8 of the necklace. Use a 5mm jump ring to attach each half of a toggle clasp to the crimp end's loop. ❖

Supply List

necklace
- paua shell donut, approx. 50 mm
- 16-in. (41cm) strand abalone shell diamonds or ovals, approx. 13 x 13mm
- 6 large-hole spacers, 4 x 5mm
- 7 x 8mm barrel-shaped spacer, hole large enough for two strands of leather
- 3 ft. (91cm) 1mm-diameter leather cord
- 8 7mm soldered jump rings
- 2 7mm jump rings
- 10 1½-in. (3.8cm) head pins
- 8 2-in. (5cm) head pins or 2 ft (61cm) 24-gauge wire
- 2 crimp ends
- hook-and-eye clasp
- E6000 glue
- chainnose and roundnose pliers
- diagonal wire cutters

bracelet
- leftover abalone shell diamonds or ovals
- 16 or more 3 x 5mm large-hole spacers
- 8 or more 6mm crystals, round or bicone
- 1½ ft. (46cm) or more 1mm-diameter leather cord
- 8 or more 6mm jump rings
- 2 5mm jump rings or split rings
- 16 or more 1½-in. head pins
- 2 crimp ends
- toggle clasp
- E6000 glue
- chainnose and roundnose pliers
- diagonal wire cutters

Autumn lariat

Fall colors flow through a graceful strand of pearls and faceted gemstones

by Candice St. Jacques

Bronze pearls acquired at one of the Tucson bead shows were the starting point for this versatile fall accessory. I chose faceted carnelian beads for contrast and mottled agates of similar size and cut to complete the basic palette. Heavy, faceted stones at each end give the lariat weight.

Wrap the lariat from the front around your neck and tie it to have a dressy accent that works well with tailored suits. Or, drape the lariat asymmetrically in front and tie it once for an artsy evening on the town.

SupplyList

- **2** 30mm faceted carnelian beads
- **2** 10mm textured gold or vermeil beads
- 16-in. (41cm) strand 8mm bronze pearls
- 16-in. strand 5mm faceted carnelian beads
- 16-in. strand 5mm faceted agate beads
- flexible beading wire, .019
- **2** size 11º seed beads
- **4** gold-filled crimp beads
- chainnose or crimping pliers
- diagonal wire cutters

B

3. Untape one end. String a 5mm gemstone, a crimp, two 5mm gemstones, another crimp, a gold bead, the carnelian bead, a 5mm gemstone, and a seed bead. Go around the seed bead and back through the beads just strung.

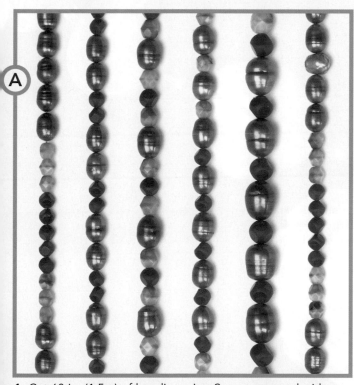

A

C

4. Tighten the wire and crimp the crimp beads (Basic Techniques, p. 10).

1. Cut 60 in. (1.5m) of beading wire. Secure one end with tape. String the pearls, carnelian beads, and agate beads for the main section of the lariat. (You'll string the beads for the ends in step 3.) Refer to the photo above to recreate my stringing sequences or create a design of your own. Leave 3 in. (8cm) of exposed wire on each end.

2. When you finish the lariat's main section, center the beads, secure the ends temporarily with tape, and check the necklace's length. Make any design or length adjustments before finishing the ends.

5. Repeat step 3 on the other end. Before you crimp, slide the beads toward the finished end to eliminate any extra space between beads. Keep the necklace flexible so it will drape well as you wear it. Crimp as before and trim the excess wire from both ends of the lariat. ❖

bracelet • 1. Determine the finished length of your bracelet. Divide the measurement in half, add 3 in. (8cm), and cut two pieces of wire to that length.

2. String a 3mm bead, a crimp bead, a 3mm bead, and the flat bead on one wire. Go back through the three beads, keeping the wire slightly loose around the flat bead. Crimp the crimp bead. Repeat on the opposite side of the flat bead.

Supply List

necklace
- 3cm top-drilled mother-of-pearl pendant
- 16-in. (41cm) strand 21mm flat teardrop-shaped, vertically drilled mother-of-pearl beads
- **38** or more 3mm Czech fire-polished beads
- 2g size 15º Delicas
- flexible beading wire, .014 or .015, gold-colored
- **2** crimp beads
- toggle clasp
- Fireline fishing line, 6 lb. test
- beading needle, #10
- G-S Hypo Cement
- chainnose or crimping pliers
- diagonal wire cutters

bracelet
- 20mm center-drilled mother-of-pearl flat bead
- leftover teardrop-shaped beads
- **14** 3mm Czech fire-polished beads
- leftover size 15º Delicas
- flexible beading wire, .014 or .015, gold-colored
- **4** crimp beads
- toggle clasp
- chainnose or crimping pliers
- diagonal wire cutters

earrings
- leftover teardrop-shaped beads
- **2** 3mm Czech fire-polished beads
- **2** 2-in. (5cm) head pins
- **2** earring wires
- roundnose pliers
- diagonal wire cutters

3. String a teardrop-shaped bead (pointed end toward the center), three 3mm beads alternating with two Delicas, and a teardrop-shaped bead on each side of the flat bead.

4. Check the fit and add or remove beads as needed. Tape one end. On the other end, string a 3mm bead, a crimp bead, a 3mm bead, and half the clasp. Go back through these beads, tighten the wire, and crimp the crimp bead (Basic Techniques). Untape the opposite end and repeat. Trim the excess wire.

earrings • String a head pin with a teardrop-shaped bead and a 3mm bead. Trim the wire to ⅜ in. (1cm) above the end bead and turn a plain loop (Basic Techniques). Open the loop on an earring wire and attach it to the head pin loop. Close the loop.

Make a second earring to match the first. ✤

Long & short of it

Mix stick pearls and round pearls for an elegant cuff

by Beth Stone

Cultivated freshwater pearls in this long, narrow shape are known as stick pearls. They come in a variety of colors, and no two are exactly alike. Their irregular form is called *baroque*, and like music of the same name, stick pearls are elegant and classy. They are also rather expensive, so use them wisely and well.

1. Determine the finished length of your bracelet, add 5 in. (13cm), and cut a piece of beading wire to that length. String a 3mm bead, crimp bead, 3mm bead, and one clasp section. Go back through the beads and tighten the wire, but do not crimp the crimp bead yet.

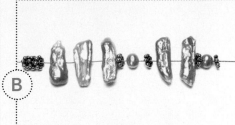

2. String three spacers, three stick pearls, spacer, round pearl, and spacer. Then string two stick pearls, spacer, round pearl, and spacer. Repeat, starting with the three stick pearls, until the bracelet is the desired length.

SupplyList

- **15** or more freshwater stick pearls
- **16** or more 6mm flat spacers
- **5** or more 6mm round pearls
- flexible beading wire, .014 or .015
- **2** crimp beads
- **4** 3mm round beads
- toggle clasp
- chainnose or crimping pliers
- diagonal wire cutters

3. String three spacers, a 3mm bead, crimp bead, 3mm bead, and the remaining clasp section. Go back through the beads and tighten the wire. Check the fit. Add or remove an equal number of beads from each end if necessary. Tighten the wires and crimp the crimp beads (Basic Techniques, p. 10). Trim the excess wire. ✤

Metal

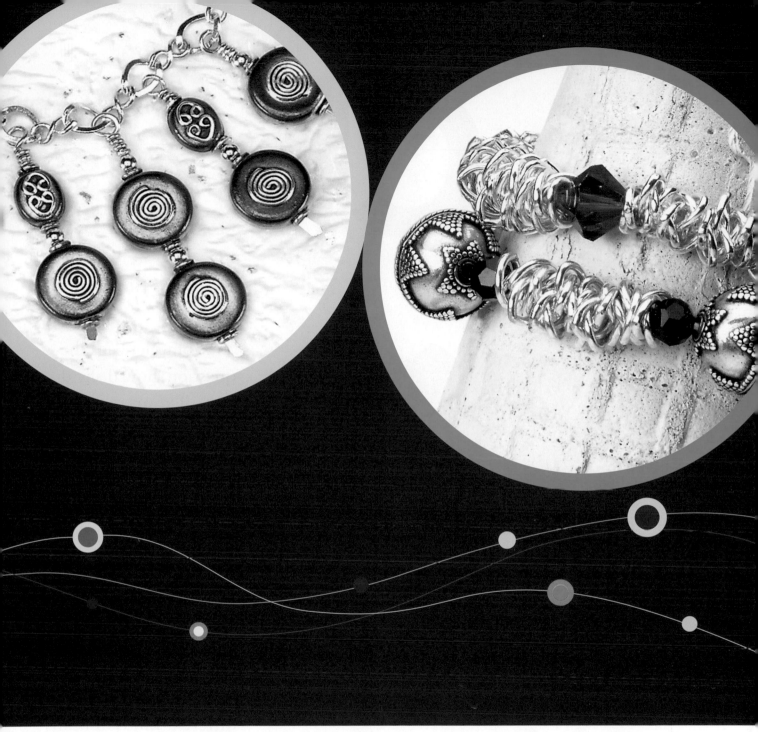

and chain

Chain

by Karin Buckingham

This bracelet begs the question, how'd she do that? The answer is deceptively simple: thread chain onto elastic and let it collapse onto itself. This creates an unexpectedly fun and fashionable bracelet that you'll be able to make in less than half an hour. Experiment with different sizes and styles of chain, add charms or dangles, or intersperse different kinds of beads to vary the results. The only struggle you'll have is whether to reveal your technique or keep it to yourself.

reaction

An unexpected technique converts chain into a stretchy bracelet

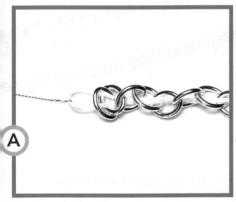

black and silver bracelet • 1. Measure your wrist, add 5 in. (13cm), and double this measurement. Cut a piece of elastic to that length. Center a twisted wire beading needle on the elastic and tape the ends together.

2. Cut four 5-in. segments of chain. String one chain segment by threading the elastic through each link. Slide the chain down the elastic as you work.

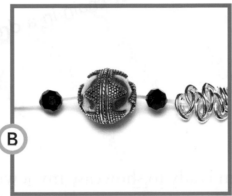

3. String a crystal, a silver bead, and a crystal. String each remaining chain segment followed by the bead sequence. Remove the tape.

4. Tie the two ends together with a surgeon's knot (Basic Techniques, p. 10). Glue the knot and slide it into the chain to hide it.

SupplyList

both bracelets
- Gossamer Floss or ribbon elastic
- twisted wire beading needle
- G-S Hypo Cement
- scissors

black and silver bracelet
- 20 in. (51cm) 5mm heavy cable chain
- 8 6mm round crystals
- 4 10-15mm silver beads

pink bracelet
- 36 in. (91cm) 5mm heavy cable chain
- 3 10mm crystals or beads

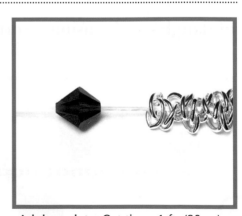

pink bracelet • Cut three 1-ft. (30cm) segments of chain. Follow the instructions for the black and silver bracelet, substituting a pink crystal for the crystals and silver beads. ❖

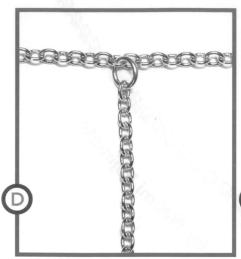

D

E

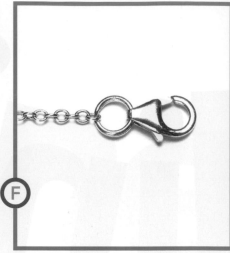

F

4. Cut a chain segment the desired length of your necklace (mine is 14½ in./37cm). Open a 3mm jump ring (Basic Techniques) and attach a 2½-in. dangle to the chain's center link. (Find the center by folding the chain in half.) Close the jump ring.

5. On each side of the center dangle, attach a 3-, 2½-, and 2-in. dangle at ⅜-in. (1cm) intervals. Count the links to determine equal intervals.

6. Check the fit. If you need to shorten the necklace, cut an equal number of links from each end. Attach a split ring to each end link. Attach a lobster claw clasp to either split ring.

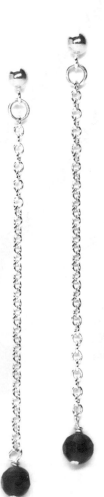

A

earrings • **1.** Cut two 2-in. chain segments.

2. String a gemstone on each of two head pins and make the first half of a wrapped loop above each bead. Attach each loop to the end link of a chain segment. Complete the wraps.

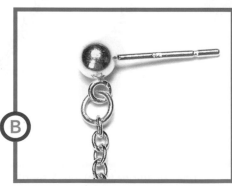

B

3. Use a 3mm jump ring to attach a dangle to the loop on the earring post. Close the jump ring. Repeat to finish the second earring. ✤

SupplyList

both projects
- chainnose and roundnose pliers
- diagonal wire cutters

necklace
- 3 ft. (91cm) or more fine-gauge cable chain
- 7 5mm round gemstones
- 7 1½-in. (4cm) head pins
- 7 3mm jump rings
- 2 split rings
- lobster claw clasp
- split-ring pliers (optional)

earrings
- 4 in. (10cm) fine-gauge cable chain
- 2 5mm round gemstones
- 2 1½-in. (4cm) head pins
- 2 3mm jump rings
- pair of earring posts with loop

Simple and streamlined

by Mindy Brooks

Make an easy chain lariat

A pair of faceted beads and a length of rolo chain are the key elements in this contemporary lariat. Although I chose synthetic gemstone briolettes, the necklace adapts easily to dangling crystals, art glass beads, and authentic gemstones. Look for teardrop, pear-shaped, or elongated beads that maintain the lariat's streamlined profile.

Supply List

- **2** 25mm or **1** 25mm and **1** 18mm horizontally drilled teardrop briolettes
- 4 ft. (1.2m) rolo chain
- 5 in. (13cm) 20-gauge wire
- chainnose and roundnose pliers
- diagonal wire cutters

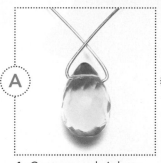

A

1. Center one briolette on a 2½-in. (6cm) length of wire and cross the wires above the bead.

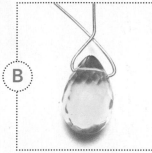

B

2. Bend one of the wire ends so it points straight up above the bead.

C

3. Wrap the angled wire around the straight one, as it completing a wrapped loop (Basic Techniques, p. 10). Trim the excess wrapping wire.

D

4. Use the straight wire to make the first half of a wrapped loop.

E

5. Slide the end link of chain into the loop.

F

6. Complete the wrapped loop and trim the excess wire. Repeat these steps to attach the remaining briolette to the other end of the chain. ❖

Chandelier earrings

Turn elegant filigree components into fabulous jewelry

by Brenda Schweder

Sometimes I'm not sure why I need to have something, but the urge to own it wins out just the same. That's what happened when I discovered the vintage metal stampings that provide the foundation for these earrings. I saw them on a buying trip, and they leapt into my arms, even though I had no specific plans for them. Although these earrings look elaborate, they are simple to make. Use vintage crystals or contemporary beads, then pick your dress and shoes to match!

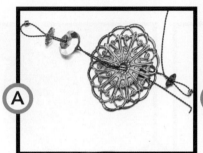

1. String a filigree stamping on beading cord from back to front and slide it close to the cord's end. String a lochrosen (flatback crystal), a 6mm margarita, and a Delica. Go back through the margarita, lochrosen, and stamping. Pick up a 5mm margarita and a Delica. Go back through the margarita. (The margarita and Delica are at the back of the stamping.)

2. Tighten the beading cord and pull the beads securely against the front of the stamping. Make sure the beads don't sag. Then tie the cord ends together with a surgeon's knot (Basic Techniques, p. 10). Glue the knot and trim the ends. Make three more lochrosen assemblies. Set aside.

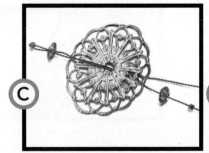

3. String a stamping and slide it close to the cord's end, as before. String a 5mm margarita and a Delica. Go back through the margarita and the stamping. String another margarita and Delica and go back through the margarita. Finish the ends as in step 2. Make three more margarita assemblies. Set aside.

4. To make the small dangles, string a cone-shaped crystal and a 5mm margarita on a head pin. Trim the head pin to ⅜ in. (1cm) above the top bead and turn a plain loop (Basic Techniques). Make three more small dangles.

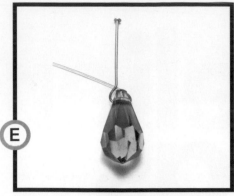

E

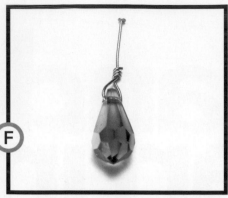

F

G

5. To make the large dangles, string a crystal drop on a head pin. Slide the bead to one-third the distance from either wire end. Bend the wire ends up over the bead, curving them with roundnose pliers.

6. Bend the longer of the two ends so it is perpendicular to the bead. Wrap the shorter end around the longer one several times.

7. Trim the longer wire to ⅜ in. above the last wrap. Turn a plain loop. Make five more large dangles.

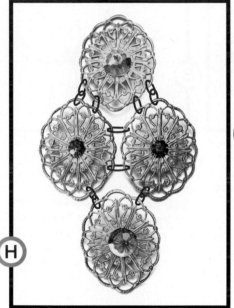

H

I

J

8. Lay out the assembled stampings so the two with 5mm margaritas in front are side-by-side. Place one lochrosen assembly above and one below them.

9. Use jump rings (Basic Techniques) to connect the stampings where indicated. Use one jump ring where the stampings are close together and two where they are farther apart. When assembled, the center row stampings will overlap slightly.

10. Attach one large dangle to the edge of the bottom stamping. Repeat on the lower edge of each center row stamping.

11. Attach a small dangle to each side of the bottom stamping. Assemble the second earring to match the first.

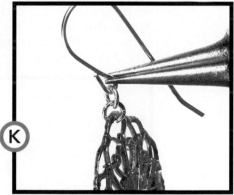

K

12. Attach a jump ring to the upper edge of the top stamping. Connect a second jump ring to the first. Open the loop on an earring wire and slide it into the top jump ring. Close the loop. Repeat to finish the second earring. ❖

Kits for these earrings are available at BrendaSchweder.com.

Supply List

- **8** oval filigree stampings, matte gold
- **6** 15mm Swarovski crystal drops, horizontally drilled
- **4** 6mm Swarovski crystal cones, vertically drilled
- **4** 8mm Swarovski lochrosens (sew-on flatback crystals)
- **4** 6mm Swarovski margaritas
- **16** 5mm Swarovski margaritas
- **16** size 15º Delicas
- **26** 4mm jump rings, gold-filled
- polyamid bead cord no. 2 with attached needle
- **10** 2-in. (5cm) head pins, gold-filled
- pair of earring wires, gold-filled
- chainnose and roundnose pliers
- diagonal wire cutters
- glue

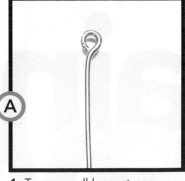

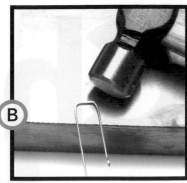

A

1. Turn a small loop at one end of two 3¾-in. (10cm) pieces of wire.

B

2. Bend each wire at a right angle 1⅜ in. (3.5cm) from the top of the loop. Make a second right angle ⅜ in. (1cm) from the first.

3. Hammer the squared-off bottom section to flatten the wire and harden it. Don't hammer the sides past ⅛ in. (3mm) from the corners.

Right-angle earrings

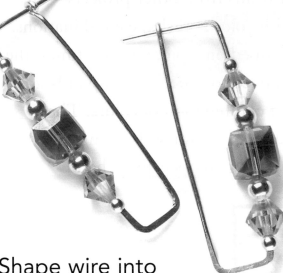

Shape wire into geometric earrings

by Wendy Witchner

Three right angles and a small loop define the basic shape of these simple earrings. Embellish them with silver or crystal beads, as shown, or adapt this design to your own style by using gemstones, glass, or clay.

C

4. To make your own spacers, wrap twisted wire around a scrap of 20-gauge wire to form a coil. Slide the coil off the wire core and cut it into four ¼-in. (6mm) sections.

D

5. String a 2.5mm bead, a coil or 6mm bead, a 3mm, an 8mm, a 3mm, a coil or 6mm, and a 2.5mm bead on each wire.

E

6. Slide the beads toward the flattened corner, as shown. Bend the wire's end at a right angle so it fits into the small loop and trim it to ½ in. (1.3cm). Hammer the right angle as in step 3. Use a metal file or emery board to smooth the cut end. Finish the second earring to match the first. ❖

Supply List

- 8 in. (20cm) 20-gauge wire
- 1 ft. (30cm) 24-gauge twisted wire or **4** 6mm beads
- **2** 6-8mm beads
- **4** 3mm round beads
- **4** 2.5mm round beads
- chainnose and roundnose pliers
- emery board or metal file
- ball-peen hammer
- small anvil or bench block
- diagonal wire cutters

Copper
concept

Link copper beads with silver chain
for a gleaming necklace and earring set

by Linda J. Augsburg

Growing up on a farm in Illinois influenced my life and
my perceptions of the world around me. The color palette
of my memory includes the brilliant blues of a summer
sky after a cleansing rain; the deep, rich shades of black
in a field just turned; the golden hues of cornstalks
rustling softly in a breeze. Writing this as fall approaches,
I recall the patchwork of autumn colors visible from our hilltop
farmstead—shades of copper, olive, straw, and soil-black—
as the crops, one by one, were harvested. The shine of metal farm
implements slicing through the copper-colored fields is forever etched on
my mind, a combination that drew me to these copper and pewter beads.

necklace • 1. Cut five 2½-in. (6cm) lengths of 20-gauge wire. Using an anvil or bench block and hammer, flatten one end of each piece of wire to form a paddle-shaped head pin.

2. String the copper and 2.5mm round beads on head pins as shown above. Make the first part of a wrapped loop (Basic Techniques, p. 10) above the end bead on each head pin.

3. To make the connecting units, cut six 2-in. (5cm) long pieces of wire and center a bead on each one. Bend each wire end into a right angle pointing in opposite directions. Make the bends 1/16 in. (2mm) from each end of the bead.

Cut four 1¼-in. (3cm) lengths of chain for the necklace sides. Cut a 5-in. (13cm) length of chain for the front. Set the rest of the chain aside.

4. Attach the dangles to the front chain as shown and complete the wrapped loops (Basic Techniques).

earrings • 1. Make two 1½-in. (4cm) long paddle-shaped head pins as in step 1 of the necklace. String a bead on each. Make the first part of a wrapped loop at the unfinished end of each head pin.

2. Cut two 2-in. long pieces of wire. String a bead on each and make the first part of a wrapped loop at both ends.

3. Cut two ¾-in. (2cm) lengths of chain. Slide the head pin onto the end link of one piece of chain. Slide a bead unit onto the link at the opposite end. Complete the wrapped loops. Open the loop on the earring finding and attach the wrapped loop to the finding. Make a second earring to match the first. ✣

5. Make the first part of a wrapped loop on each side of the connecting units. Slide one end of a unit through the end link on the front chain section. Slide the other end through the end link on a side chain section. Complete the wrapped loops.

Join another unit and side chain section to this end of the necklace. Then add one more unit to the end link of chain. Complete the wrapped loop on all but the last connector unit.

Repeat this step on the opposite end of the front section.

6. Check the length of the necklace. Cut two 1¼-in. or longer lengths of chain. Attach one chain to each unfinished connecting unit. Complete the wrapped loops.

To attach the clasp, use split rings to connect each soldered jump ring to an end chain link.

7. Complete the wrapped loop on the crystal unit. Slide the unfinished loop of an art bead unit into the wrapped loop. Complete the wrapped loop.

8. Continue connecting art bead units and crystal units to complete the front of the necklace. When you connect the last crystal unit, complete the wrapped loops on both of the unit's ends. Remove the tape from the unfinished strand, string a crimp bead, and go through the loop on the crystal unit. Finish this end as in step 6. ✤

SupplyList

- **3** art glass or other focal beads (beads in silver necklace by Joel Park, galleryeas1@cs.com; beads in gold necklace by Jeff Plath, glassriverbeads.com)
- **4** 8mm Swarovski crystals, round
- **8** 4mm Swarovski crystals, bicone
- **12** 5mm faceted rondelles
- **126** 6mm spacers
- **6** 8mm bead caps
- **8** 5mm bead caps
- 30 in. (76cm) 22-gauge wire
- flexible beading wire, .014 or .015
- **4** crimp beads
- S-hook clasp with **2** soldered jump rings
- chainnose and roundnose pliers
- diagonal wire cutters

Simply stated

Embellish metal findings to make dangling earrings • by Mindy Brooks

These very easy earrings start with a pair of metal filigree findings. Use plain and wrapped loops to add crystals, gemstones, or glass bead dangles.

If you like your jewelry with more drama than these offer, you'll love Brenda Schweder's chandelier earrings on page 100. Mine are a simpler, scaled-down version, clearly more suitable for casual occasions than for a night at the Academy Awards.

crystal earrings • 1. Center a bicone on a head pin. Trim the head off the wire. Make the first half of a wrapped loop (Basic Techniques, p. 10) on each side of the bead.

String a teardrop on a head pin and make the first half of a wrapped loop above the bead.

Make two of each unit.

2. Slide one of the bicone's wire loops into the finding's upper loop. Complete the wraps (Basic Techniques) on both wire loops.

3. Slide the teardrop's wire loop into the finding's bottom loop and complete the wraps.

4. Open the loop on an earring wire and slide the bicone's upper loop into it Close the earring's loop. Make a second earring to match the first.

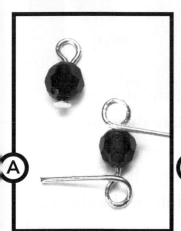

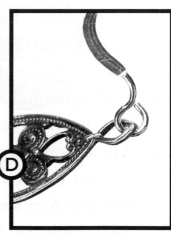

carnelian earrings • 1. String a carnelian bead on a head pin, trim the wire to ⅜ in. (1cm) above the bead, and turn a plain loop (Basic Techniques). Make five more plain-loop units.

Center a bead on a head pin. Trim the head off the wire. Make the first half of a wrapped loop on each side of the bead. Make a second wrapped-loop unit.

2. Slide the loop of a plain-loop unit into the unfinished loop of a wrapped-loop unit. Finish the wraps. Slide the unfinished loop through the finding's center loop. Finish the wraps.

3. Open the loops (Basic Techniques) on two plain-loop units and connect them to the finding's outer loops. Close the loops.

4. Open the loop on an earring wire and connect it to the finding's upper loop. Close the loop. Make a second earring to match the first. ❖

Supply List

both projects
- chainnose and roundnose pliers
- diagonal wire cutters

crystal earrings (left)
- 2 4mm bicone crystals
- 2 6mm teardrop crystals
- 4 2-in. (5cm) head pins

- pair of filigree findings
- pair of earring wires

carnelian earrings (right)
- 8 6mm faceted round gemstones, carnelian
- 8 2-in. head pins
- pair of filigree findings
- pair of earring wires

C

4. On each side of the center section, string a spacer bar to keep the strands aligned, if desired. Continue stringing beads until the bracelet is complete.

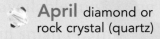

D

5. Finish the bracelet with a spacer bar, if desired. String a 3mm spacer, a crimp bead, a 3mm spacer, and half the clasp on each strand. Go back through the last beads strung. Tighten the wires but do not crimp the crimp beads. Repeat on the other end. Check the fit and add or remove beads evenly from each end, if necessary. Crimp the crimp beads (Basic Techniques, p. 10), and trim the excess wire. ✤

Supply List

(materials will vary)

- 4.5 or 5.5mm alphabet beads
- 3 or 4mm spacer beads (one more per strand than the number of letters in each name)
- gemstones or crystals representing birth month(s)
- bead caps, spacers, and spacer bars, as desired

- 3mm spacer beads, **4** for each strand
- flexible beading wire, .014 or .015
- crimp beads, **2** for each strand
- clasp
- chainnose or crimping pliers
- diagonal wire cutters

January garnet or rose quartz

February amethyst or onyx

March aquamarine or bloodstone

April diamond or rock crystal (quartz)

May emerald or chrysoprase

June alexandrite, moonstone, or pearl

July ruby or carnelian

August peridot or sardonyx

September sapphire or lapis

October opal or tourmaline

November topaz or citrine

December turquoise or zircon

Shortcuts

Readers' tips to make your beading life easier

1 sturdy strands

Instead of using a larger-diameter flexible beading wire to string heavy beads, I use two strands of .014 or .015 wire. If one strand breaks, the second provides reinforcement and holds the beads together. Just make sure the beads at the ends of the piece have holes large enough to accommodate four strands of wire.
– Dee Martin, via e-mail

2 the key to shopping

When I have some beads for a project, but need additional components, I string the beads on a head pin, make a wrapped loop, and attach the head pin to my keychain. The keychain keeps the beads accessible, and seeing my beads every day motivates me to complete my project. – Linda Stark, Jacksonville, FL

3 in the cards

When I'm considering colors for a project, I go to the hardware store and select an assortment of paint chips. Since they are portable, reusable, and easy to sort, chips help me see a variety of possible colors and design arrangements. – Charlee Cole, Los Angeles, CA

4 seed bead solution

To make a bail (hanging loop) for a large-hole bead, string size 8º or 10º seed beads on a head pin to fit inside the larger bead. The seed beads will prevent the head pin from moving around and help the large bead hang evenly.
– Anne Peterson, via e-mail

5 crimping compromise

For foolproof crimping, I use both crimping and chainnose pliers. First, I use the lower grooves in the crimping pliers to create the fold in the crimp bead. Then, I use chainnose pliers to fold the crimp in half. This method creates a secure crimp with less likelihood of breaking adjacent beads.
– M.R. Miller, Evanston, IL

6 carried away

For compact and portable organization, store your seed beads in a wooden utensil carrier. Each compartment holds 15 or more tubes, so you can keep 90 to 100 tubes within reach. Plus, the carrier keeps the tubes upright—helpful if you work with several different colors at one time.
– H.C. Mercer, via e-mail

7 space that measures up

I designed my own inexpensive beading surface using textured foam shelf liner and a cloth tape measure. Cut approximately 28 in. (71cm) of liner and staple a 2-ft. (61cm) length of tape measure across the bottom. The pad is inexpensive, portable, and beads won't roll off the surface.
– Martha Wilderman, St. Peters, MO

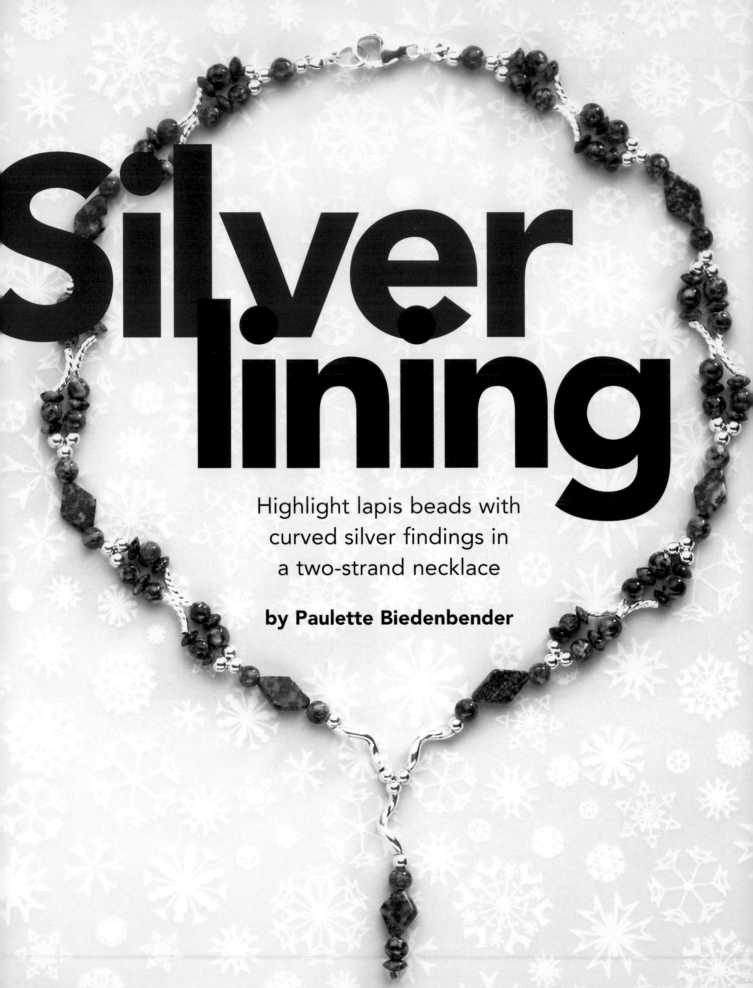

Silver lining

Highlight lapis beads with
curved silver findings in
a two-strand necklace

by Paulette Biedenbender

Curved silver findings add textural interest as they bring this necklace from one strand to two and back again. Make this necklace with lapis lazuli as I did, or find these same shapes in another stone.

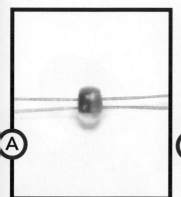

1. Cut two 30-in. (76cm) lengths of Fireline and center a seed bead on both strands.

2. Bring all four ends together and string a button-shaped lapis, round lapis, diamond-shaped lapis, another round, 3mm silver bead, curved tube bead, and another 3mm.

3. Separate the four strands into two pairs. String a 3mm silver bead onto each pair.

4. String a curved tube bead, 3mm silver bead, round lapis, diamond-shaped lapis, round lapis, and a 3mm silver bead on each end of the necklace.

5. Separate the two strands of one pair and string a 3mm silver bead on each. On the outer strand, string a button-shaped lapis, round lapis, and a button-shaped lapis.

On the inner strand, string a round, button, and round. String the two-strand tube with the lower end on the outer side of the necklace.

On the outer strand, string a round lapis, button, round, and 3mm silver bead. On the inner strand, string a button, round lapis, button, and 3mm silver bead.

6. String a 3mm silver bead, round lapis, diamond-shaped lapis, round lapis, and 3mm silver bead over both strands. Repeat steps 5-6 on the other end of the necklace.

7. Repeat the two patterns until the necklace sides are approximately 7 in. (18cm) or the desired length. Allow at least 3 in. (8cm) for finishing the ends.

8. To attach the clasp, string a round lapis, 3mm silver bead, and a bead tip. Separate the strands and string a seed bead on one of them. Tie a surgeon's knot (Basic Techniques, p. 10) over the bead, tightening the knot as you slide the bead into the bead tip.

9. Glue the knot. When the glue is dry, closely trim the excess Fireline and close the bead tip with chainnose pliers. Repeat on the other end of the necklace. ❖

Supply List

- 16-in. (41cm) strand 12mm diamond-shaped lapis lazuli
- 16-in. strand 4mm round lapis
- 16-in. strand 4mm button-shaped lapis
- 6 13.4mm two-strand beads, silver (Rio Grande, 800-545-6566, riogrande.com)
- 3 13mm curved tube beads (Rio Grande)
- **44** 3mm round silver beads
- **2** seed beads
- **2** bead tips
- Fireline fishing line, 6lb. test
- G-S Hypo Cement
- chainnose pliers

Link metal washers to chain for a modern necklace, bracelet, and earring collection

by Brenda Schweder

After finding these nifty metal washers, I wanted to create pieces that emphasized their open design. My first attempts were crude, manifesting themselves as a knotted metal lump. After struggling with a complex design, I opted for simplicity instead. The necklace, bracelet, and earrings require only two sizes and two colors of washers, and the technique is equally manageable—attach the washers to chain with jump rings, add a clasp, and go!

A

B

necklace • 1. Determine the finished length of your necklace (mine is 16 in./41cm) and cut a piece of chain to that length. Open a jump ring (Basic Techniques, p. 10) and string on one or two washers.

2. Find the center link by folding the chain in half.

3. Loop the jump ring through the center link of the chain and close it.

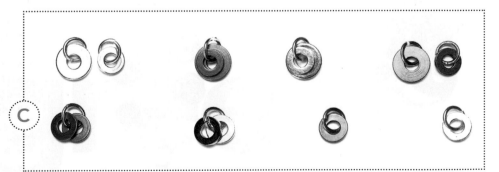

C

4. On each side of the center, use jump rings to attach one or two washers to subsequent chain links. (Make sure each dangle hangs downward from the chain.) Vary the colors and sizes, and include combinations of paired and single washers. Attach the washers to an equal number of links on each side of the center. (The washer section of my necklace extends 15 links on each side of the center.)

A

B

C

necklace • 1. To make the connecting units, cut 20 2½-in. (6.4cm) pieces of wire. Center a 6mm crystal on a wire, and make the first half of a wrapped loop (Basic Techniques, p. 10) on each end of the crystal. Make 20 units.

2. Slide a crystal unit's loop into an opening on the centerpiece filigree just right of center. Complete the wraps.

3. Slide the remaining loop into a smaller filigree's loop. Complete the wraps.

4. Slide a crystal unit's loop into the small filigree's other loop and complete the wraps. Repeat steps 3 and 4 twice more. End with a crystal unit.

5. Repeat steps 2 through 4 on the other side of the centerpiece starting just left of center.

D

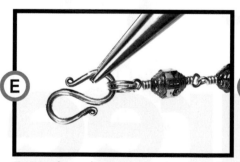

E

F

6. Add crystal units to each end until you reach the desired length of your necklace (mine is 18 in./46cm).

7. Attach a split ring to the last crystal unit's loop on each end. Slide the S-hook clasp through one of the split rings.

8. To make a fringe unit, cut a 2-in. (5cm) length of wire. At one end, make a loop large enough to hang loosely from the bottom of the centerpiece. Slide the loop through one of the center openings.

G

H

9. Complete the wraps and thread a 4mm bead on the wire. Turn a plain loop (Basic Techniques) below the bead.

10. String a 4mm bead on a 2-in. piece of wire and turn a plain loop above and below the bead. Open a loop at one end and attach it to the end loop of the previously attached fringe unit. Close the loop.

11. Repeat steps 8 through 10 until you've made four fringes in the lengths shown in photo H.

Supply List

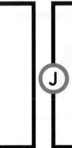

I

J

12. To make the end units, string a 4mm bead on a head pin and turn a plain loop above the bead. Make three more end units.

13. Open the loop of an end unit and slide it through the last loop on a fringe. Close the loop. Repeat on the remaining three fringes.

A

earrings • 1. String a crystal and two 4mm beads on a head pin.

B

2. Insert the head pin into the filigree cone. Make a wrapped loop above the cone.

C

3. Open the loop on an earring wire and attach the earring. Make a second earring to match the first. ❖

Combine silver and gemstones for ethnic appeal

I find something comfortably appealing about the balance and strength of a symmetrical design. A round silver medallion is the perfect starting point for a symmetrical necklace incorporating the Southwest flavors of stone and silver. The necklace at left uses Botswana agate and silver accents; the necklace at right, turquoise and yellow quartz.

Southwestern
symmetry

by Anne Nikolai Kloss

(A)

1. Determine the finished length of your necklace, add 6 in. (15cm) for finishing, and cut a piece of beading wire to that length. (Mine is 16 in./41cm and has a 2-in./5cm chain extension.) Center three 4mm beads, the medallion, and three more 4mm beads on the beading wire.

Supply List

- **16-in. strand 8mm gemstones**
- **16-in. (41cm) strand 4mm gemstones**
- **15** 6mm accent beads
- **five-strand medallion (Ashes to Beauty Adornments, 505-899-8864)**
- **50** 3mm silver spacers
- **6 in. (15cm) rolo chain with 2mm links**
- **2 in. (5cm) chain with 4mm links**
- **6** head pins
- **5** 3mm jump rings
- **flexible beading wire, .014 or .015**
- **2** crimp beads
- **split ring**
- **S-hook clasp with soldered jump ring**
- **chainnose or crimping pliers**
- **roundnose pliers**
- **diagonal wire cutters**

126

B

2. On each side of the necklace, string a spacer, 6mm bead, spacer, 8mm bead, spacer, 6mm bead, spacer, and six 4mm beads. Repeat this sequence twice on each side. String 4mm beads and spacers to within 1 in. (2.5cm) of the desired length.

C

3. On one end, string a crimp bead, a 4mm bead, and the clasp. Go back through the last three beads and tighten the wire, leaving a small loop around the jump ring. Crimp the crimp bead (Basic Techniques, p. 10) and trim the excess wire.

D

E

4. On the other end, string a crimp bead, a 4mm bead, and a split ring. Finish as in step 3. To make the necklace length adjustable, attach 2 in. (5cm) of chain to the split ring.

5. String a 4mm bead on a head pin. Begin a wrapped loop (Basic Techniques) above the bead and slide the end link of chain into the wire loop. Complete the wrapped loop.

F

G

6. Cut five pieces of rolo chain: one 12-link segment, two 10-link segments, and two 8-link segments. Use a jump ring (Basic Techniques) to connect each chain segment to the medallion as shown, with the longest segment in the center.

7. To make the dangles, arrange a graduated design of beads and spacers on five head pins.

H

I

8. Cut the wire to ⅜ in. (1cm) above the top bead on each head pin. Turn a plain loop (Basic Techniques).

9. Attach each dangle to its corresponding chain on the medallion. ✤

6. Slide the end link of a 3-in. chain segment into unit A, as shown. Complete the wrapped loop. Repeat on the other side.

7. Complete unit D's top loop. Slide the end link of the 3-in. chain, the top loop of unit D, and the end link of the remaining 3-in. chain into unit C's bottom loop. Complete the wraps on unit C's loop.

8. Slide one unit E through the center link of the 3-in. chain segment and the second link from the center of the upper strand. Carefully maneuver the chain into the loop and finish the wrap.

9. Add two more unit Es to this connection. Make sure to go through the link on the lower chain only. Complete the wraps. Repeat steps 8 and 9 on the other side of unit C.

SupplyList

- **5** 6mm crystal rondelles
- **15** 6mm round glass beads
- **19** 4mm bicone crystals
- **4** 3mm spacers
- **9** 1½-in. (4cm) head pins
- **3** ft. (91cm) 20-gauge wire
- **2** in. (5cm) 2.9 mm rolo chain
- **2** ft. (61cm) 6mm figure-8 chain
- clasp
- chainnose and roundnose pliers
- diagonal wire cutters

10. To make the chain dangles, cut one 1-in. (2.5cm) and two ½-in. (1.3cm) chain segments from rolo chain. Slide each end link of chain through a unit E. Complete the wrapped loops.

11. Slide the chain segments through unit D's lower loop, as shown. Complete unit D's wrapped loop. ❖

Charm school

Personalize a bracelet with silver charms

by Naomi Fujimoto

In the past, charm bracelets reflected the efforts of dedicated collectors. Now, you don't have to wait for years of birthdays and special events to put one together. Simply buy a handful of charms and attach them to a ready-made bracelet. Charms are commonly available in sterling silver, gold, pewter, and enamel. Traditional bracelets showcase your favorite things; mine includes charms that represent my rambunctious dog, Ginger, jewelry-making, basketball, and cheeseburgers. Another option is to put together a vanity version with purse, shoe, and makeup charms, accented with pearls. Whether you want to represent what's closest to your heart or to convey a specific theme, charm bracelets are both fun and timeless.

Gemstones

necklace • 1. Determine the finished length of your necklace (mine is 17½ in./44cm), add 6 in. (15cm), and cut a piece of beading wire to that length.

String a nugget, a bead ring, a crimp bead, a spacer, and half the clasp. If you're stringing 3mm beads individually, don't string one in place of the ring; its hole is too small to get the wire through a second time. Go back through these beads, tighten the wire, and crimp the crimp bead (Basic Techniques). Trim the excess wire.

3. To finish the necklace, string a crimp bead, a spacer, and the remaining clasp half. Go back through these beads, the bead ring, and the nugget. Tighten the wire and crimp the crimp bead. If the crimp slides into the ring as you tighten the wire, make a small hole in a piece of cardboard and restring the crimp, spacer, and clasp with the cardboard between the ring and the crimp. Then tighten the wire and crimp the crimp bead. Remove the cardboard and trim the excess wire.

2. String an alternating pattern of nuggets and bead rings or nuggets and single beads. Check the length and add or remove beads as needed. End the strand with a ring, if using them, or with a nugget if using 3mm beads individually.

Supply List

both projects
- chainnose or crimping pliers

necklace
- 16-in. (41cm) strand gemstone nuggets (amazonite)
- 16-in. strand 3mm round gemstones (rhodonite)
- flexible beading wire, .018 or .019
- 2 crimp beads
- 2 3mm spacer beads
- clasp
- Fireline fishing line, 6 lb. test or Nymo D (optional)
- beading needle, #12 (optional)
- G-S Hypo Cement (optional)

bracelet
- leftover gemstone beads
- **30-35** 6mm silver spacers
- **2** 3mm round silver beads
- flexible beading wire, .014 or .015
- **2** crimp beads
- lobster claw clasp
- 6mm split ring or soldered jump ring

Contributing editor Anne Nikolai Kloss designed this bracelet for us using beads left over from the necklace. She added silver spacers to provide the necessary length.

bracelet • 1. Cut a length of beading wire 5 in. (13cm) longer than your wrist measurement. String a crimp, a round silver bead, and the lobster claw clasp. Go back through the beads, tighten the wire, and crimp the crimp bead.

2. String spacers, 3mm beads, and nuggets as shown or design your own bracelet using leftover gemstones and other beads you have on hand.

3. Check the length and add or remove beads as needed. String a crimp bead, a 3mm bead, and a split ring or soldered jump ring. Go back through these beads, tighten the wire, and crimp the crimp bead. Trim the excess wire at both ends. ✤

Match gemstones with a striking pendant

A black-and-white necklace is the perfect accessory to bridge your wardrobe from winter to spring. Dalmatian jasper offers a subtle combination of creamy white and muted black, and the rainbow obsidian pendant lends an air of elegance to this classic design.

by Karin Buckingham

Fashion statement

SupplyList

- 10 x 30mm (approx.) focal bead
- 16-in. (41cm) strand 8mm round gemstones
- 16-in. strand 6mm round gemstones
- **96** 4mm crystals
- flexible beading wire, .014 or .015
- **4** crimp beads
- **8** 3mm round spacer beads
- two-strand clasp
- chainnose or crimping pliers
- diagonal wire cutters

1. Determine the finished length of the inner strand of your necklace (mine is 18½ in./47cm), add 6 in. (15cm), and cut a piece of wire to that length. Cut a second wire 2½ in. (6cm) longer.

2. Center the focal bead on the longer wire. On each side, string an alternating pattern of one crystal and one 8mm bead, stopping within 1½ in. (3.8cm) of the desired length from each end.

3. On the shorter wire, string an alternating pattern of a 6mm bead and a crystal, stopping within 1½ in. (3.8cm) of the desired length from each end.

4. String a 6mm bead, a 3mm spacer, a crimp bead, a spacer, and half the clasp on each strand on both ends. Go back through the last beads strung.

5. Check the fit and add or remove beads as necessary. Tighten all four wires and crimp the crimp beads (Basic Techniques, p. 10). Trim the excess wire. ❖

Gemstone round

by Laurie D'Ambrosio

This necklace is a compilation of beads of different shapes. Beautiful round gemstones along the length of the necklace are accented with square spacers. These, in turn, complement the round and disc-shaped beads at the necklace's center. Strung in a longer, 26-in. (67cm) length, the necklace is a perfect partner for winter's bulky knits.

Supply List

- 16-in. (41cm) strand 8mm round gemstone beads (tigerskin jasper or red tigereye)
- **48** 2-3mm cube-shaped metal spacers
- **8** 8mm round accent beads (jasper or carnelian)
- **5** 14-15mm discs (jasper or carnelian)
- **4** 10mm round accent beads (leopardskin jasper or agate)
- **2** 10mm discs (stone or metal)
- flexible beading wire, .014 or .015
- **2** crimp beads
- **2** size 11º seed beads
- clasp
- chainnose or crimping pliers
- diagonal wire cutters

up

String an easy necklace using stones in several shapes

A

1. Determine the finished length of your necklace, add 6 in. (15cm), and cut a piece of beading wire to that length.

String a 10mm disc. String a 14mm disc, an 8mm accent bead, a 10mm bead, and 8mm bead. Repeat three more times, starting each pattern with a 14mm disc. End with a 14mm disc and a 10mm disc.

B

2. String an alternating pattern of 8mm gemstone beads and cube-shaped spacers on each end until the necklace is the desired length. End with a spacer.

C

3. String a crimp bead, a seed bead, and one half of the clasp. Go back through the beads just strung and a few adjacent beads. Crimp the crimp bead (Basic Techniques, p. 10) and trim the excess wire.

D

4. Repeat step 3 on the other end. Before crimping, make sure there are no gaps between beads. ❖

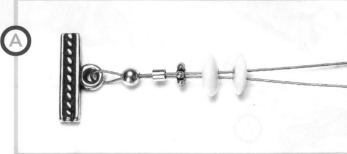

bracelet • 1. Determine the finished length of the bracelet, add 5 in. (13cm), and cut a piece of beading wire to that length. String two discs, a spacer, crimp bead, 3mm bead, and half the toggle clasp. Go back through the beads and tighten the wire, but don't crimp the crimp bead yet.

2. String a spacer, rondelle, spacer, 8mm bead, spacer, rondelle, and spacer.

3. String ¾ in. each of discs and pearls (see necklace, photo A).

4. String a spacer, 8mm bead, spacer, rondelle, spacer, nugget, spacer, rondelle, spacer, 8mm bead, and spacer (see necklace, photo B). End with ¾ in. each of pearls and discs.

5. Repeat step 2, then string two discs, a spacer, crimp bead, 3mm bead, and the remaining section of the clasp. Go back through the last beads strung and check the fit. Add or remove an equal number of beads from each side, if necessary. Tighten the wires on both ends, crimp the crimp beads, and trim the excess wire.

earrings • 1. String a head pin with an 8mm bead, spacer, and two pearls. Make a wrapped loop (Basic Techniques) above the end bead.

2. Open the loop on an earring wire and attach the beaded unit. Make a second earring to match the first. ❖

by Naomi Fujimoto

Autumn elements

Surround a raku bead with gemstones

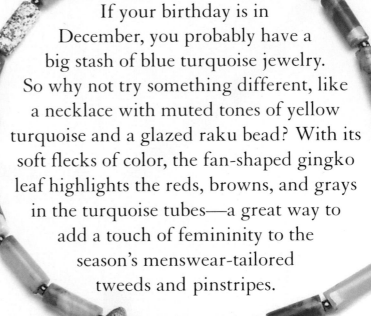

If your birthday is in December, you probably have a big stash of blue turquoise jewelry. So why not try something different, like a necklace with muted tones of yellow turquoise and a glazed raku bead? With its soft flecks of color, the fan-shaped gingko leaf highlights the reds, browns, and grays in the turquoise tubes—a great way to add a touch of femininity to the season's menswear-tailored tweeds and pinstripes.

A

1. Determine the finished length of your necklace (mine is 17 in./43cm), add 6 in. (15cm), and cut a piece of beading wire to that length. Center a raku bead on the beading wire. If the bead's hole is large, string a few seed beads to fill it.

B

2. On each side of the pendant, string 8 in. (20cm) of seed beads and tubes in an alternating pattern. Check the fit and add or remove beads, if necessary. End with a seed bead.

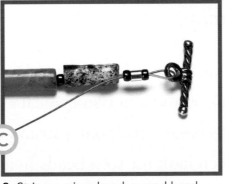

C

3. String a crimp bead, a seed bead, and one section of the toggle clasp. Go back through the last beads strung, tighten the wire, and crimp the crimp bead (Basic Techniques, p. 10). Trim the excess wire. Finish the other end in the same way.

Supply List

- raku bead (Emerald Stacy of RAMA, at Knot Just Beads, 414-771-8360)
- 16-in. (41cm) strand 4 x 10mm turquoise tubes
- 2g size 11º seed beads, reddish brown
- flexible beading wire, .014 or .015
- **2** crimp beads
- toggle clasp
- chainnose or crimping pliers
- diagonal wire cutters

Jaded

Seed beads and a jade pendant accent an aventurine necklace

by Naomi Fujimoto

Whip up this necklace to wear with your white tee shirt, jean jacket, and a not-so-cynical attitude. Choosing the beads is easy: pick out a strand of gemstone tubes, then look for seed beads in a few different colors. Most colors will work—the effect is subdued once you combine them with tube beads.

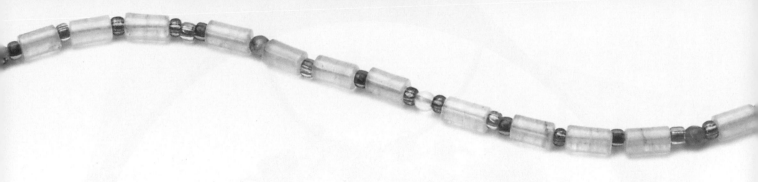

1. Determine the finished length of your necklace (mine is 16 in./41cm), add 6 in. (15cm), and cut a piece of beading wire to that length.

To make a pendant, string a gemstone nugget onto a head pin. (If you are not making a pendant, skip to step 3 and begin stringing.) Make a wrapped loop (Basic Techniques, p. 10) and trim the excess wire.

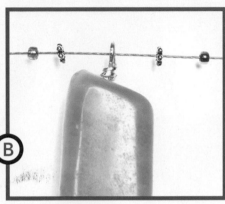

2. Center the pendant on the beading wire. On each side, string a spacer and a seed bead.

Supply List

necklace
- 16-in. (41cm) strand 3 x 5mm gemstone tubes
- 16-in. strand 2mm round gemstones, jasper
- size 11° seed beads, 1g in each of three colors (purple, red, rust)
- flexible beading wire, .014 or .015
- **2** crimp beads
- lobster claw clasp
- 5mm split ring or soldered jump ring
- chainnose or crimping pliers
- diagonal wire cutters

optional pendant
- gemstone nugget, jade
- **2** or more silver spacers
- 2½-in. (6cm) head pin
- chainnose and roundnose pliers

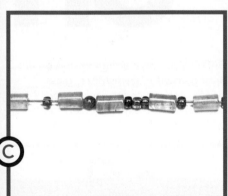

3. String approximately 7¾ in. (20cm) of assorted beads on each side of the pendant. If you are not including a pendant, string 14 in. (36cm) or more of beads from end to end. Intersperse the tube beads with various colors and sizes of round gemstones and seed beads. Use single beads as well as combinations of two to five beads between each tube. End each strand with two or more seed beads.

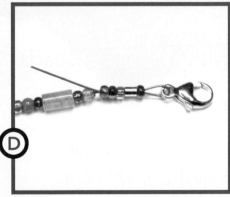

4. String a crimp bead, a seed bead, and the clasp on one end of the beading wire. Go back through the seed bead, crimp, and several seed beads. Tighten the wire so it forms a small loop around the clasp. Crimp the crimp bead (Basic Techniques) and trim the excess wire.

Repeat on the other end, using a split ring or soldered jump ring in place of the clasp. ❖

Tie one on

Knot a casual necklace with amethyst beads

by Paulette Biedenbender

A little wild, a lot of fun, but polished—sometimes you need a necklace with those qualities. That's the feeling I get from this leather, linen, and amethyst piece. The medley of gemstone shapes gives you the freedom to create a variety of arrangements. You'll probably spend more time arranging your beads than stringing and knotting them, so be sure to choose beads with holes large enough to accommodate the waxed linen or thread.

Before you begin stringing, design an arrangement of gemstones, glass beads, and cubes for each strand. The stone slices are asymmetrical, so play with them to find a pleasing mix.

necklace • 1. Cut three 18-in. (46cm) strands of waxed linen thread. To make a lark's head knot as shown above, fold one linen thread in half, drape it over the leather cord, and pull the ends through the fold.

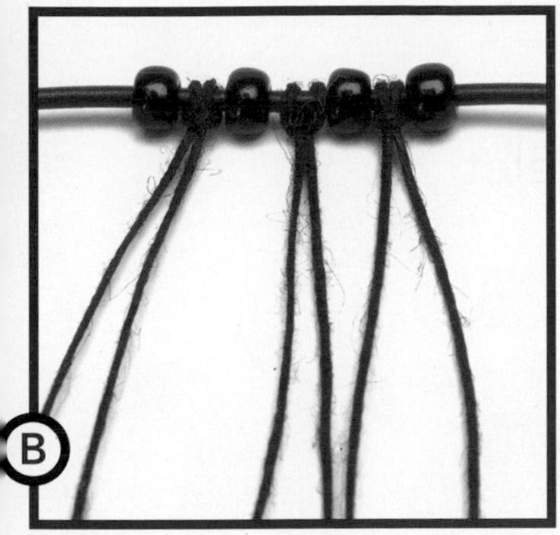

2. String a 6mm bead on each side of the knot. Use the lark's head knot to attach each of the two remaining threads on the cord. String a 6mm bead after each knot.

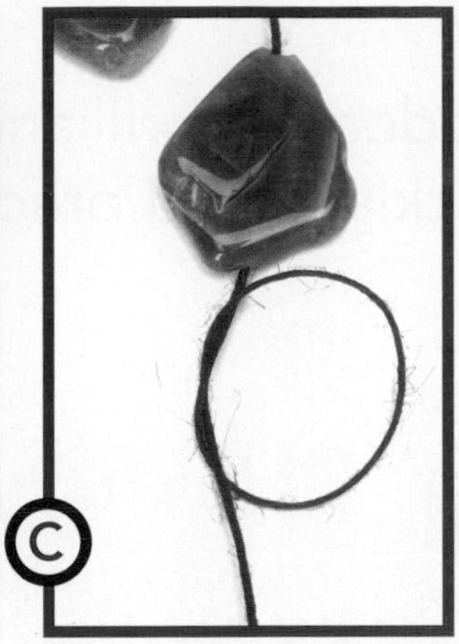

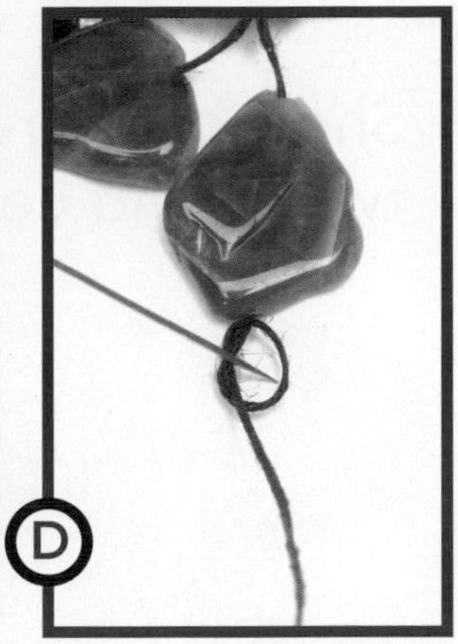

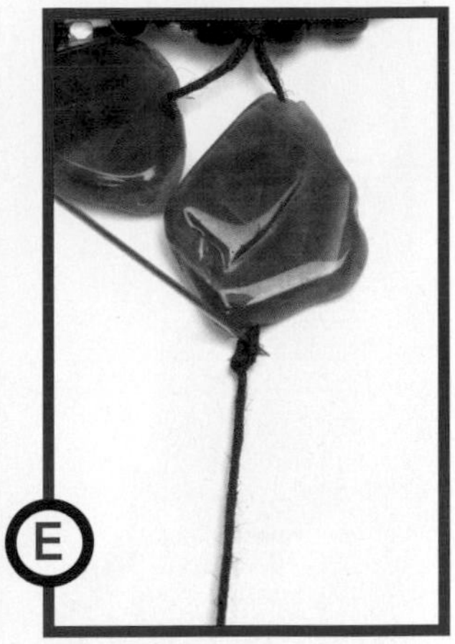

3. Working from your arrangement of beads, string a gemstone slice or other bead into position on one of the waxed threads. Make a loose overhand knot (Basic Techniques, p. 10) below the bead (C). Insert your needle or beading awl into the knot and slide the knot against the stone (D). Tighten the knot as you position it (E). (To undo a knot, insert the awl into it and slide it away from the bead.)

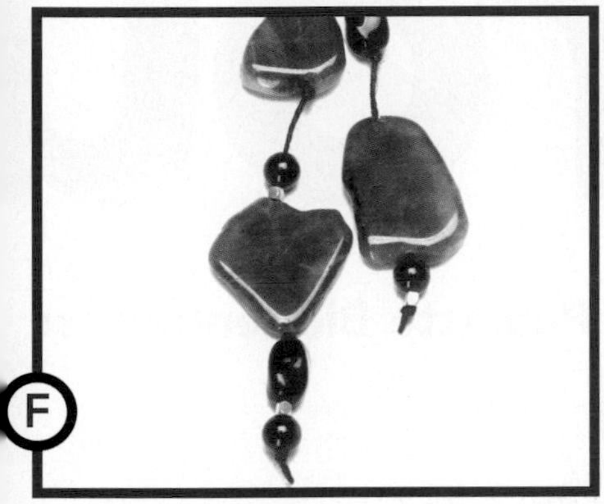

4. String the remaining beads for this strand, knotting them singly or in groups, as desired. Make an overhand knot below the last bead. String the remaining strands, knotting them where desired.

When you're satisfied with the arrangement, trim the bottom threads about ¼ in. (6mm) below each of the end knots.

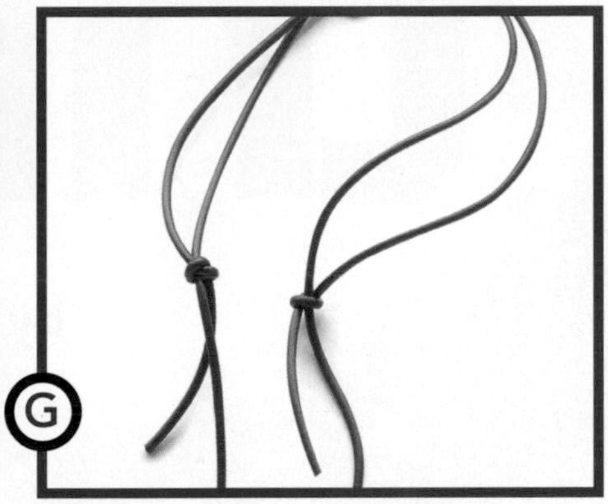

5. To complete your necklace, tie each end of leather cord around the opposite end with an overhand knot. To adjust the length, slide the knots close together to lengthen the necklace or pull them apart to shorten it.

Supply List

necklace

- 16-in. (41cm) strand gemstone slices, amethyst
- **6** 12mm twisted oval glass beads
- **6** 6mm round beads, amethyst
- **4** 6mm glass beads (large holes)
- **10** 2.5mm cube-shaped beads
- **1** spool waxed linen thread
- 30 in. (76cm) 2mm leather cord
- awl or thin knitting needle
- scissors

earrings

- **2** leftover gemstone slices
- **4** 2.5mm cube-shaped beads
- **2** 2-in. (5cm) head pins
- **2** earring wires
- roundnose and chainnose pliers
- diagonal wire cutters

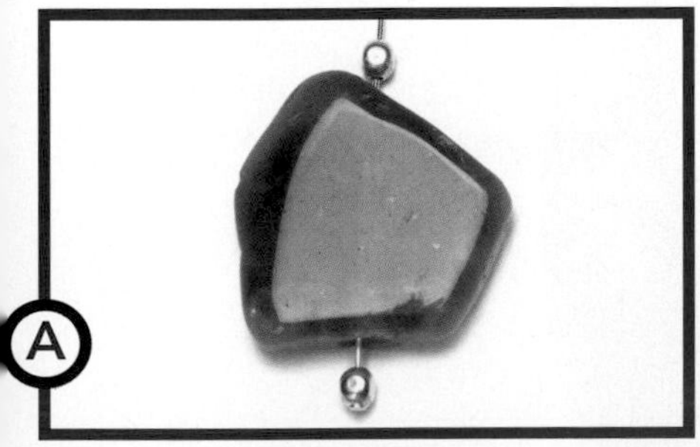

earrings • **1.** String a cube bead, a gemstone slice, and another cube on a head pin. Make a wrapped loop above the top bead (Basic Techniques).

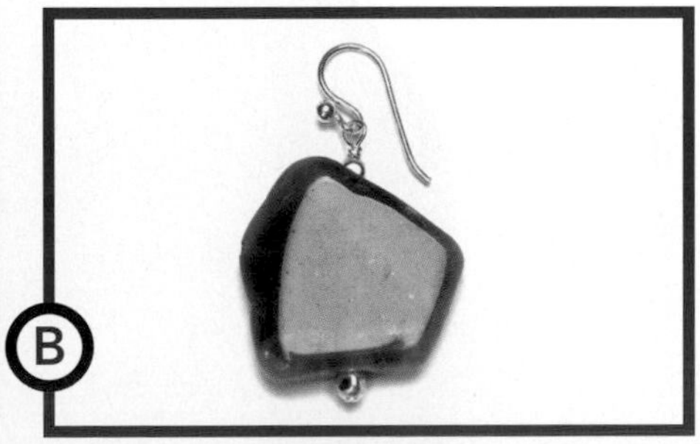

2. Open the earring wire slightly and attach the loop of the head pin. Close the earring wire. Make a second earring to match the first. ✤

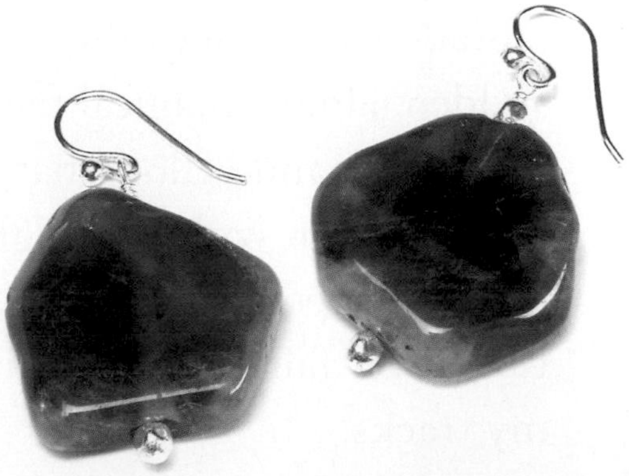

Show off labradorite's brilliance in a
two-strand necklace and bracelet

Shining throu

by Paulette Biedenbender

When I shop for beads, bright
and bold colors are more my style
than muted grays. So, what makes
the blue-gray gemstone
labradorite so appealing? It's the
sudden, almost magical flash of
blue, gold, and yellow that
appears from within, as light
strikes the polished surface,
that never fails to stop me in
my tracks.

SupplyList

both projects
- flexible beading wire, .014 or .015
- roundnose and chainnose pliers
- diagonal wire cutters
- crimping pliers (optional)

necklace
- 19 x 25mm (approx.) gemstone nugget, pietersite
- **3** 16-in. (41cm) strands labradorite, 10mm ovals
- **2** 16-in. strands 5mm labradorite, faceted rondelles
- 6-in. (15cm) strand 3mm round crystals
- **8** 3mm round spacer beads
- **2** 2 x 8mm two-hole decorative spacers
- **2** crimp beads
- 3-in. (8cm) head pin
- two-strand toggle clasp

bracelet
- leftover labradorite, rondelles and ovals
- **8** 3mm round spacer beads
- 2 x 8mm two-hole decorative spacer
- **4** crimp beads
- two-strand slide clasp

A

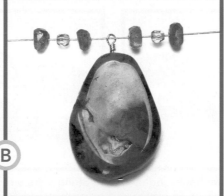

B

C

3. String an oval, rondelle, oval, rondelle, crystal, and rondelle. Repeat pattern once more. Repeat the pattern on the other side of the pendant.

D

4. On each end, string a two-hole spacer through its bottom hole. Tape the ends.

necklace • 1. To make the pendant, string the gemstone nugget onto a head pin. Make a wrapped loop above the bead (Basic Techniques, p. 10).

2. Determine the finished length of your necklace (my shortest strand is 17½ in./44cm), add 6 in. (15cm), and cut one piece of beading wire to that length. Cut a second piece 1 in. (3cm) longer. Center the pendant on the longer strand. String a rondelle, crystal, and rondelle on each side of the pendant.

157

E

F

G

5. To add the inner strand, pass one end of the remaining beading wire through the top hole of either spacer. String an oval, rondelle, oval, rondelle, crystal, and rondelle. Repeat the pattern three more times. String an oval, rondelle, and oval. Go through the remaining spacer.

6. String a rondelle, crystal, and rondelle on the inner strand. On the outer strand, string an oval. String the pattern in step 3 on both ends of both strands until the necklace is the desired length. Repeat on the other end of the necklace. Tape the ends and check the fit. Add or remove an equal number of beads from each end, if necessary.

7. Untape the wires on one end. String a 3mm round spacer, crimp bead, and spacer on each strand. Pass each wire through a toggle loop and go back through the last beads strung. Tighten the wires and crimp the crimp beads (Basic Techniques). Trim the excess wire. Repeat with the other half of the clasp.

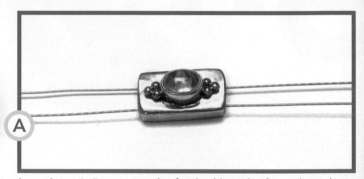

A

bracelet • 1. Determine the finished length of your bracelet, add 5 in. (13cm), and cut two pieces of beading wire to that length. Center a two-hole spacer on both strands.

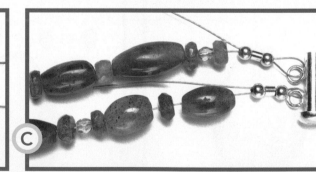

B

C

2. On the top strand, string the pattern shown beginning with a rondelle. On the bottom strand, begin with an oval. String each strand until 3 in. (8cm) from the end.

Repeat on the other side of the spacer, but begin with an oval on the top strand and a rondelle on the bottom.

3. String a 3mm round spacer bead, crimp bead, and spacer on each strand. Pass each strand through the respective loops of the slide clasp and go back through the last beads strung. Do not crimp the crimp beads. Repeat on the other end of the bracelet, making sure the clasp sections are in the correct position (or the clasp won't close).

Check the fit and add or remove beads on each end, if necessary. Tighten the wires and crimp the crimp beads. Trim the excess wire. ❖

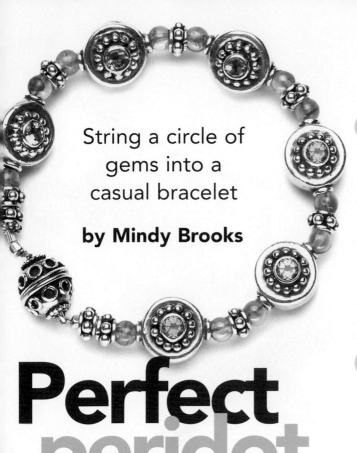

String a circle of gems into a casual bracelet

by Mindy Brooks

Perfect
peridot

When you stumble across a bead that's hard to resist, the challenge can be finding the right place to use it. Not having a project in mind kept me from buying these decorative silver beads for some time. It wasn't until I saw them in peridot, my birthstone, that I knew how easy it would be to feature them in a simple bracelet design.

Supply List

- **6-8 12mm diameter silver beads with peridot** (Fire Mountain Gems, 800-355-2137)
- **12-16 4mm round peridot beads**
- **9-11 3 x 6mm silver spacer beads**
- **2 2.5mm silver beads**
- **flexible beading wire, .014 or .015**
- **2 crimp beads**
- **magnetic clasp**
- **chainnose or crimping pliers**
- **diagonal wire cutters**

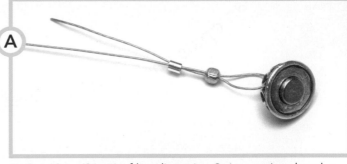

1. Cut 12 in. (31cm) of beading wire. String a crimp bead, a 2.5mm bead, and half the clasp. Go back through the bead and the crimp. Tighten the wire to form a small loop around the clasp. Crimp the crimp bead (Basic Techniques, p. 10).

2. String two spacers and slide them next to the crimp, covering the wire tail. Follow the stringing sequence shown here or design a pattern of your own. String enough beads to encircle your wrist comfortably.

3. String two spacers, a crimp, a 2.5mm bead, and the remaining clasp section. Go back through the last four beads.

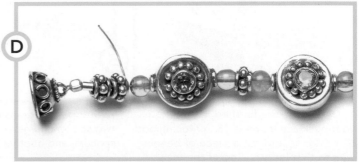

4. Tighten the wire, leaving a small loop around the clasp. Crimp the crimp bead and trim the excess wire from both ends. ❧

Peruvian opals and sterling silver shine in an eye-catching necklace

(A)

1. Determine the finished length of your necklace (mine is 18 in./46cm), add 6 in. (15cm), and cut a piece of beading wire to that length. Center the focal bead on the wire and string two 4mm beads and a spacer on each side. Tape one end.

(B)

2. String a flat gemstone nugget, two spacers, large accent bead, two spacers, and another nugget.

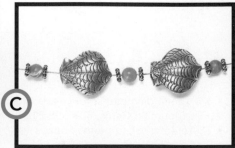

(C)

3. String a spacer, 4mm bead, spacer, and the smaller accent bead. Repeat. End with a spacer, 4mm bead, and spacer.

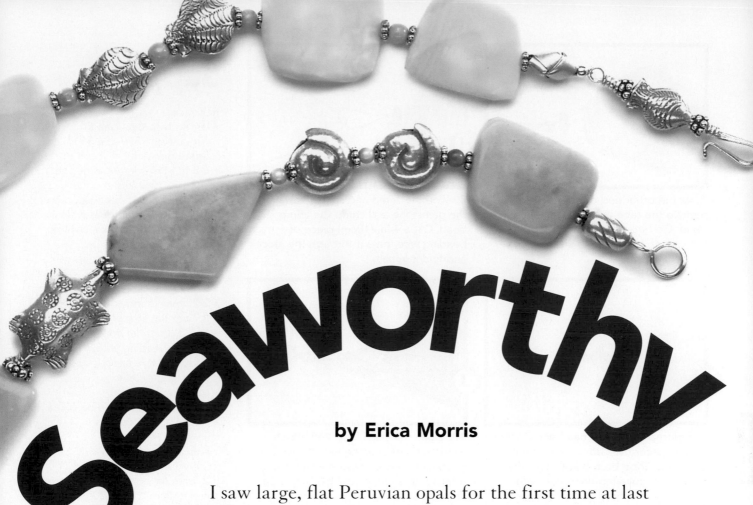

Seaworthy

by Erica Morris

I saw large, flat Peruvian opals for the first time at last year's gem shows in Tucson, Arizona. These highly polished stones are luxuriously smooth and comfortable against the skin. To complement the stones, I chose handmade Thai silver sea creatures. Choosing beads and stones of the same thickness helps the finished piece lay flat around your neck. This necklace is versatile—sporty enough for daytime attire and sophisticated enough for evening wear. Enjoy it as you sail away on a late winter cruise.

4. String a flat gemstone nugget and a spacer. Tape the end. Repeat steps 2 through 4 on the other end of the necklace. Check the fit and add or remove beads on each side, if necessary.

5. String a large-hole silver bead, a crimp bead, 2.5mm round spacer, and the hook end of the clasp (see p. 162 to make this clasp). Go back through the last beads strung, tighten the wire, and make a folded crimp (Basic Techniques, p. 10). Don't trim the excess wire.

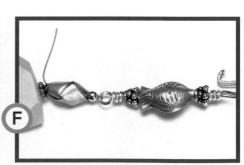

6. Slide the wire tail through the large-hole bead. Slide all the beads toward the clasp and maneuver the crimp inside the large-hole bead. The large hole should be flush against the round bead. Trim the excess wire.

G

7. At the other end of the necklace, remove the tape and string a crimp bead. Go back through the crimp and the spacer, leaving a ¾-in. (2cm) loop.

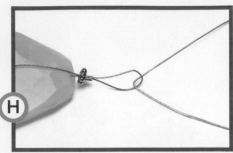

H

8. Slide the crimp and spacer toward the gemstone and crimp the crimp bead. Cut a 4-in. (10cm) piece of beading wire, pass it through the loop, and fold it in half.

I

9. String a large-hole bead and 2.5mm round spacer over both ends of the 4-in. wire. Slide both beads over the two loops, covering the crimp with the large-hole bead. Slide the spacer against it. A small loop of beading wire will extend beyond the spacer. Remove the 4-in. piece of wire.

J

10. Open the clasp loop and attach it to the loop of beading wire. Close the clasp loop. If your clasp doesn't open, attach a split ring to the beading wire. Trim the excess wire.

Supply List

necklace
- large silver focal bead (Tiger Tiger, 510-236-9917, tiger-tiger.com)
- **6-8** flat Peruvian opal nuggets, approx. 20 x 30mm (770-696-5321, ebeadshop.com)
- **10-12** 4mm round Peruvian opals
- **2** silver accent beads, approx. 14 x 28mm
- **4** silver accent beads, approx. 10 x 15mm
- **2** 10mm large-hole silver beads
- **2** 2.5mm round spacer beads
- **8** 7mm flat spacer beads
- **16-20** 3mm flat spacer beads
- flexible beading wire, .024
- hook-and-eye clasp (or custom clasp, see below)
- split ring (optional)
- chainnose and crimping pliers
- diagonal wire cutters

custom clasp (optional)
- 10mm silver accent bead
- **2** 3mm round spacer beads
- 7 in. (18cm) 18- or 20-gauge sterling silver wire
- chainnose and roundnose pliers
- diagonal wire cutters

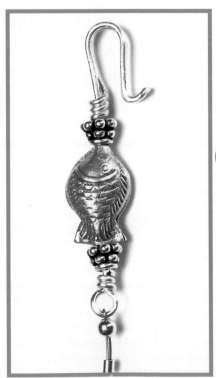

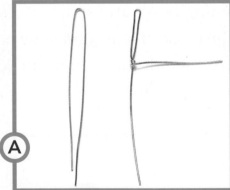

A

custom clasp • 1. Cut a 7-in. (18cm) length of 18- or 20-gauge wire and bend it in half.

2. Cross half the wire over the other about 1½ in. (4cm) below the fold. Wrap the bent piece around the straight wire twice. Trim the wire close to the wraps.

B

3. String a spacer, an accent bead, and a spacer on the straight wire. Make a wrapped loop (Basic Techniques) below the spacer and trim the excess wire. Pinch the wires together above the accent bead with chainnose pliers. Make a slight bend at the tip of the fold.

4. Use roundnose pliers to curve the loop downward, making sure the bent tip faces outward as shown. ✤

Pastel persuasion

Subtle shades accent a birthstone necklace

by Naomi Fujimoto

Since November's traditional birthstone, topaz, is not readily available as beads, I worked with citrine, which is often listed as a substitute. The heft, golden color, and unusual facets of these nuggets appealed to me. When combined with faceted stone buttons, rose crystals, and silver Delicas, the result is sparkly, not fussy—perfect for the cerebral Scorpio.

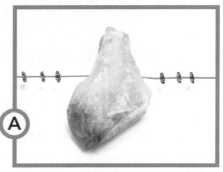

1. Determine the finished length for your necklace (mine is 16 in./41cm), add 6 in. (15cm), and cut a piece of beading wire to that length. Center three spacers, the citrine nugget, and three spacers on the wire.

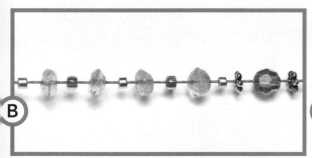

2. On each side of the pendant, string citrine buttons alternating with Delicas and salmon seed beads as shown. Begin with a Delica. When you've strung eight buttons, add a spacer, 4mm round crystal, and a spacer. Repeat the pattern three or more times, until you have strung approximately 7 in. (18cm) of beads on each end. End with a Delica or seed bead. Check the fit and add or remove beads, as needed.

3. String a crimp bead, a Delica or seed bead, and the clasp. Go back through the last three beads and tighten the wire. Crimp the crimp bead (Basic Techniques, p. 10) and trim the excess wire. Finish the other end in the same way, substituting a jump ring for the clasp. ❖

SupplyList

- citrine nugget, approx. 2 x 3cm
- 16-in. (41cm) strand 4mm-diameter faceted citrine buttons
- **8-12** 4mm round Swarovski crystals, light rose champagne
- **50-60** Delicas, silver
- **50-60** size 11º seed beads, salmon
- **22-30** 3mm flat silver spacers
- flexible beading wire, .014 or .015
- **2** crimp beads
- lobster claw clasp
- soldered jump ring
- chainnose or crimping pliers
- diagonal wire cutters

Imperial
lariat

Highlight a gemstone necklace with a jade donut

by Candice St. Jacques

If the Olympics had begun in China, the winners would have been designated by a different hierarchy of materials: ivory for third place, gold for second, and jade for first. That's how the imperial court actually rewarded athletes, because jade—a highly treasured stone of many virtues—was considered gentle, sensitive, persevering, moral, and beautiful, not to mention priceless. With this in mind, I selected a jade donut to anchor this lariat. You can use other gemstone donuts just as effectively.

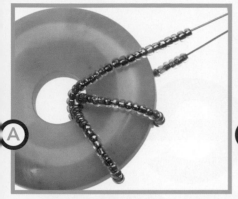

1. String 4 in. (10cm) of seed beads on a 40-in. (1m) length of beading wire and slide them to one end. Wrap the beads around the donut several times and bring the wires together. Add or remove beads as needed to create close-fitting loops around the donut.

2. String ten 8mm beads, a crimp bead, and a 4mm bead onto both wire ends. Slide them next to the seed beads. Tighten the wire and crimp the crimp bead (Basic Techniques, p. 10). Trim the excess wire.

Supply List

- 16-in. (41cm) strand 8mm button-shaped faceted gemstones, fluorite
- 16-in. strand 4mm round faceted gemstones, amethyst
- 3.2cm gemstone donut, minimum hole size 12mm, jade
- 10g size 11º seed beads
- flexible beading wire, .014 or .015
- 2 crimp beads
- chainnose or crimping pliers
- diagonal wire cutters

3. String 4mm beads, 8mm beads, and seed beads in various patterns as shown or design your own bead sequences. Continue until you're about 4 in. from the end of the strand.

4. String a crimp followed by 1 in. (2.5cm) or so of gemstone beads. End with a seed bead. Turn, skip the seed bead, and go back through the last beads strung. Continue through a few beads past the crimp.

Tighten the beads along the entire strand so the lariat is flexible but no wire shows between beads. Crimp the crimp bead as before and trim the excess wire. ❖

The nature of things

Combine slices of turquoise with coral discs and textured silver for a bold, asymmetrical necklace and bracelet

by Arlene Schreiber

Yellow turquoise, red coral, and textured Bali silver are pronounced components on their own, but in combination, they create a striking piece of jewelry. Begin by choosing interesting and sizeable semi-precious stones. Using a larger clasp not only adds to the design, but allows you to turn a plain jump ring into a decorative finish.

necklace • 1. Determine the finished length of your necklace (mine is 17 in./43cm), add 6 in. (15cm), and cut a piece of beading wire to that length. String the clasp, a barrel-shaped bead, crimp bead, and a coral disc. Go back through all the beads strung, tighten the wire to form a small loop, and crimp the crimp bead (Basic Techniques, p. 10). Trim the excess wire.

2. String a bead cap, a 4mm round, a 10mm round, a 4mm round, and a bead cap as shown. Repeat this pattern two more times, starting with a coral disc.

3. String a turquoise chunk, bead cap, 4mm round, and barrel-shaped bead. Repeat the pattern in step 2, starting with a coral disc, three times.

D

4. String a turquoise chunk, bead cap, 4mm round, and barrel-shaped bead. Repeat the pattern in step 2, beginning with a coral disc, five times.

E

5. String a turquoise chunk, a bead cap, 4mm round, bead cap, crimp bead, a 3 x 4mm spacer bead, and soldered jump ring. Go back through the last three beads strung, tighten the beading wire, and crimp the crimp bead. Trim the excess wire.

Rock Solid

Use an easy wire technique to connect gemstone nuggets

by Lea Rose Nowicki

Don't pass this project by
simply because you haven't tried
working with wire. This fast necklace is an
excellent way to get started, and the results look
undeniably professional, even for a first-timer.
Practice your loops with inexpensive copper wire from a
hardware or craft store. When you can turn a round loop, buy
sterling silver, nickel silver, or gold-filled wire—all are good choices for
jewelry-making. Choose chunky beads in your favorite color, then find a
clasp with a narrow tip that will easily hook onto a wire loop.

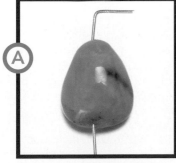

1. String a nugget on the end of the wire. Bend the wire at a right angle about ½ in. (1.3cm) from the tip.

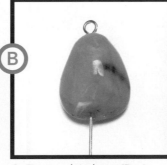

2. Turn a plain loop (Basic Techniques, p. 10) above the nugget. Trim the wire below the nugget to ½ in.

3. Turn another loop below the nugget.

4. Prepare enough nuggets to fit comfortably around your neck. Make one loop on one nugget slightly larger than the rest. (You'll use this nugget on the end opposite the clasp.) Set aside one stone without wire.

5. Open a loop on one nugget and attach it to the loop on another. Close the loop. Connect the remaining nuggets in the same way.

Attach the nugget with one larger loop to either end of the necklace using its smaller loop.

6. Open the loop on the nugget at the opposite end of the necklace and attach the clasp. Close the loop.

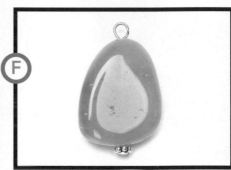

7. To make the dangle, string a 3mm flat spacer and the reserved nugget on a head pin. Trim the wire to ½ in. and make a loop above the bead.

8. Open the large loop on the end without the clasp and attach the dangle.

9. To wear the necklace, connect the clasp to the large loop. ❖

Supply List

- 16-in. (41cm) strand 20-25mm gemstone nuggets, chrysoprase (green), faceted citrine (yellow)
- 2-in. (5cm) head pin
- 3mm flat spacer
- 3 ft. (90cm) 20-gauge wire
- S-hook or hook-shaped clasp
- chainnose and roundnose pliers
- diagonal wire cutters

Shortcuts

Readers' tips to make your beading life easier

1 home plate
I use inexpensive paper plates as bead trays, because their fluted edges keep beads from rolling away. When finished, I simply bend the plate in half and pour the beads into a container. The plates also work well as rests for open glue tubes, keeping the stickiness away from my work surface. – DIANE UNDERWOOD, VIA E-MAIL

2 cutting chain
To get two even pieces of chain from one longer one, fold the chain in half and string each of the end links onto a head pin. You'll have either one or two links hanging at the bottom. If you have one link, cut it. If you have two, cut both. You'll be left with equal lengths, without having to count the links.
– TARYN YAGER-SAYLES, ROSEVILLE, MN

3 deviled egg tray
Use an oyster plate or deviled egg tray to separate beads by color and type when working on a project. Egg trays have many sections, and their depth makes them especially well-suited to organizing seed beads or small crystals and gemstones.
– LYNNE SHELDON, DEERFIELD, IL

4 not just for babies
Although glass baby food jars have long been used as storage containers, the new plastic ones with snap-on tops are also a great option. They are clear, stackable, easy to carry, and best of all, unbreakable.
– MARY MARZANO, DELRAY BEACH, FL

5 jump rings in a pinch
If you are finishing a piece of jewelry and realize that you need a soldered jump ring, you can substitute a link of chain. Simply cut the next-to-last link of chain and use the last link in place of a soldered jump ring.
– B. WELLS, VIA E-MAIL

6 tying up loose ends
It's easy to make an adjustable closure on a leather necklace. First, make sure your cord is long enough to slip over your head when knotted. Next, string the ends through a large-hole bead in opposite directions and tie an overhand knot at each end. Put the necklace on and pull the ends to adjust its length.
– PEGGY THOMAS, RIDGEFIELD, CT

A pa

Enhance a gemstone
necklace with an
eye-catching centerpiece

by **Mindy Brooks**

ssion for pendants

Pendants in shell, stone, metal, clay, and glass are front and center on stylish necklaces, and it's an easy look to accomplish. To hang a pendant, you need a *bail*, the loop that connects the pendant to the necklace strand. For the shell pendant, which has a center hole, seed beads in a matching color form a delicate loop. Another way to create a bail is with wire, which suits the jade pendant with its hole near the edge.

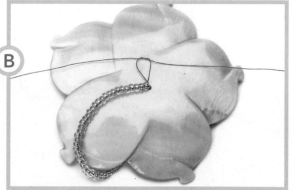

1. To string a bead loop, thread a needle with 12 in. (30cm) of Fireline and string enough seed beads to reach loosely from the center front to the center back. Go through the center hole from front to back, continue through the seed beads again in the same direction as before, and bring the needle through to the back of the shell.

2. Tighten the Fireline to pull the beads into a circle around the pendant. Tie the ends together with a surgeon's knot (Basic Techniques, p. 10) and glue the knot. Go through a few beads past the knot to hide the ends and trim the excess thread. Repeat to hide the remaining tail. Skip to step 6 to begin stringing.

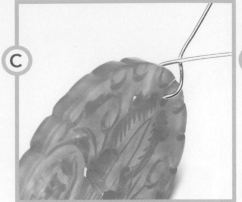

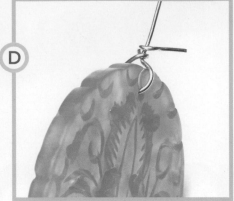

3. To make a wire loop, slide 1½ in. (4cm) of wire through the pendant's hole. Bend the wire so it curves around the stone.

4. Wrap the shorter wire around the longer one as if completing a wrapped loop (Basic Techniques). Trim the excess wire close to the wraps.

5. Make the first half of a wrapped loop about ⅛ in. (3mm) above the wraps made in step 4. Complete the wraps.

6. Determine the finished length for your necklace (mine are 16 in./41cm plus chain), add 6 in. (15cm), and cut a piece of beading wire to that length.

Center the pendant on the beading wire. String a symmetrical pattern of beads and spacers on each side of the pendant.

SupplyList

both necklaces
- flexible beading wire, .014 or .015
- chainnose or crimping pliers
- diagonal wire cutters

rhodonite (pink) necklace
- 16-in. (41cm) strand 9mm gemstone barrel beads, rhodonite
- center-drilled pendant, carved shell
- **36** or more 3mm silver spacers
- **50** (approx.) size 11º seed beads to match pendant color
- **6** 2.5mm silver beads or **6** size 11º seed beads
- lobster claw clasp with jump ring
- **2** in. (5cm) chain or soldered jump ring
- **2** crimp beads
- Fireline fishing line, 6 lb. test or Nymo D
- beading needle, #10
- G-S Hypo Cement

turquoise (green) necklace
- 16-in. strand 12 x 18mm (approx.) gemstone nuggets, turquoise
- top-drilled pendant, jade
- **4** in. (10cm) 20-gauge wire
- **10g** size 8º seed beads
- **2** crimp beads
- S-hook clasp
- **2** in. (5cm) chain or **1** soldered jump ring
- roundnose pliers

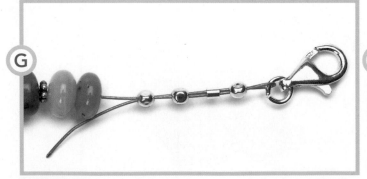

7. Check the length and add or remove beads as needed. To attach the clasp, string two 2.5mm beads (or seed beads), a crimp bead, and another 2.5mm bead. Go through the clasp and back through these four beads. Tighten the wire to form a small loop around the clasp and crimp the crimp bead (Basic Techniques). Trim the excess wire.

8. To finish the other end, string two 2.5mm beads (or seed beads), a crimp bead, and another 2.5mm bead as in step 7. Go through the end link of chain or soldered jump ring and back through the last beads strung. Tighten the wire and crimp the crimp bead. Trim the excess wire. ❖

A triangular stone pendant highlights
a two-strand necklace

by Carole Rodgers

Art has always been a part of my life—I've
been a silversmith, art therapist, art teacher,
and writer of jewelry articles and books. I
also enjoy traveling and make an RV trip to
Arizona every January. We camp at
Quartzite, where the many gem and mineral
mines supply flea-market goods. After this
rendezvous for rockhounds, we move on to the
gem shows in Tucson, where unusual items like
the yellow jade pendant in the shape of a Chinese
axe often turn up.

On the
double

*The yellow jade
necklace measures
26 in. (66cm); the
agate necklace
measures 20 in.
(51cm). For a
balanced look, keep
the pendant size
in mind when
determining a
suitable necklace
length.*

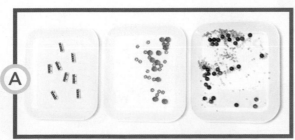

1. Pour your beads onto a few trays to save time
when you string. Determine the finished length for
your necklace, add 6 in. (15cm), and cut two
pieces of Fireline to that length. Thread a needle
on each end of both strands. Set one strand aside.

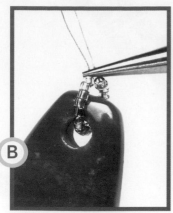

B

2. Center the pendant on one strand of Fireline. Thread enough seed beads to form a loose ring around the top of the pendant.

C

3. String both needles through a 4mm bead, seed bead, 4mm bead, seed bead, 4mm bead, and a spacer.

D

4. Repeat these steps with the remaining strand of Fireline so you have two identical bead sequences attached to the pendant.

String a two-holed bead or spacer bar as shown. If your two-holed beads have different front and back sides, lay the piece flat to help you string them correctly.

E

5. Using both needles on one side, string a spacer, 4mm bead, seed bead, 4mm bead, spacer, 6mm bead, and another spacer.

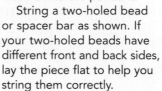

F

6. Separate the two strands and string three seed beads on each.

G

7. On one of these strands, string a 4mm bead, seed bead, 4mm bead, spacer, 6mm bead, spacer, 4mm bead, seed bead, and 4mm bead.

H

8. String the pattern on the adjacent strand, then string a two-holed bead.

I

J

K

L

9. Repeat steps 7 and 8 four or more times, until you are approximately 2 in. (5cm) short of the desired length.

To string the other side of the necklace, repeat steps 5 through 9.

10. On one strand, string the pattern in step 7, then three seed beads. Repeat on the adjacent strand.

11. String both strands through a spacer, 6mm bead, spacer, 4mm bead, seed bead, and bead tip.

M

N

12. On one strand, string a seed bead. Tie a surgeon's knot (Basic Techniques, p. 10) around the bead. Glue the knot and trim the ends to ⅛ in. (3mm). Gently close the bead tip using chainnose pliers or your fingers.

Repeat steps 10 through 12 on the other side of the necklace.

O

P

13. Attach a split ring to each half of a toggle clasp.

14. Use chainnose or roundnose pliers to attach the hook of each bead tip to a split ring. ❖

Supply List

both necklaces
- Fireline fishing line, 8lb. test
- **4** beading needles, #10
- G-S Hypo Cement
- chainnose or roundnose pliers
- split ring pliers
- small trays or dishes

yellow jade necklace
- axe-shaped pendant drilled front to back, yellow jade
- **2** 16-in. (41cm) strands 4mm round yellow quartz beads
- 16-in. strand 6mm round sponge coral beads
- **13** 12 x 18mm two-holed sponge coral beads

- 10g size 14º seed beads, reddish brown
- **68** 4mm gold spacers
- **2** clamshell bead tips
- **2** 5mm split rings
- toggle clasp

brown agate necklace
- triangular pendant drilled front to back, agate
- **2** 16-in. (41cm) strands 4mm round jasper beads
- **32** 6mm round Swarovski crystals, indicolite
- **11** 4 x 11mm two-holed silver spacer bars
- 10g seed beads, silvery blue
- **60** 3mm silver spacers
- **2** clamshell bead tips
- **2** 5mm split rings
- toggle clasp

Rich shades of gemstones
combine with silver accents
in these chunky necklaces

by Lea Rose Nowicki

I love to display a special gemstone pendant by pairing it with beads in a coordinating color. Select beads that reveal subtle gradations of color—for example, carnelian contains shades of orange, yellow, and brown. Or, try blue lace agate, amethyst, aventurine, or rose quartz. To complete the necklace, select spacers that enhance the pendant's setting.

Karma carnelian

necklace • 1. Determine the finished length of your necklace (mine are 15½ in./39cm), add 6 in. (15cm), and cut a piece of beading wire to that length. Tape one end and center the pendant on the wire.

2. String an alternating pattern of ovals, 4mm beads, and spacers as shown. Repeat the eight-bead pattern once more, then string an oval bead, a 4mm bead, and another oval. For a longer necklace, continue the pattern or string a few round silver beads. Tape the end.

3. Remove the tape from the other end. String a 2.5 or 3mm round and position the pendant's bail (its hanging loop) over it. (The round bead allows the pendant and surrounding beads to hang evenly.) Repeat step 2. Check the length of the necklace and add or remove beads as needed.

4. String a 2.5 or 3mm round, a crimp bead, round, and one section of the clasp.

5. Go back through the last beads strung and tighten the wire so it forms a small loop around the clasp. Crimp the crimp bead (Basic Techniques, p. 10) and trim the excess wire.

6. Repeat steps 4 and 5 on the other end.

earrings • 1. String a head pin with an oval, a spacer, and a 4mm round.

2. Make a wrapped loop (Basic Techniques) above the round bead.

3. Open an earring wire and attach the bead unit. Close the earring wire. Make a second earring to match the first. ❖

Supply List

necklace
- 16-in. (41cm) strand 10 x 14mm oval gemstones, carnelian or blue lace agate
- 16-in. strand 4mm round gemstone beads, faceted carnelian, or 4mm round crystals, shadow crystal
- gemstone pendant with bail, carnelian or chalcedony
- **4-6** 4 x 8mm disc-shaped spacers, silver
- **4-6** 5 x 6mm barrel-shaped spacers, silver
- **5** or more 2.5 or 3mm round silver beads
- flexible beading wire, .014 or .015
- **2** crimp beads
- toggle clasp
- chainnose or crimping pliers
- diagonal wire cutters

earrings
- **2** 10 x 14mm gemstones left over from necklace
- **2** 4mm round beads left over from necklace
- **2** 4mm silver spacers
- **2** 2½-in. (6cm) head pins
- pair of earring wires
- chainnose and roundnose pliers
- diagonal wire cutters

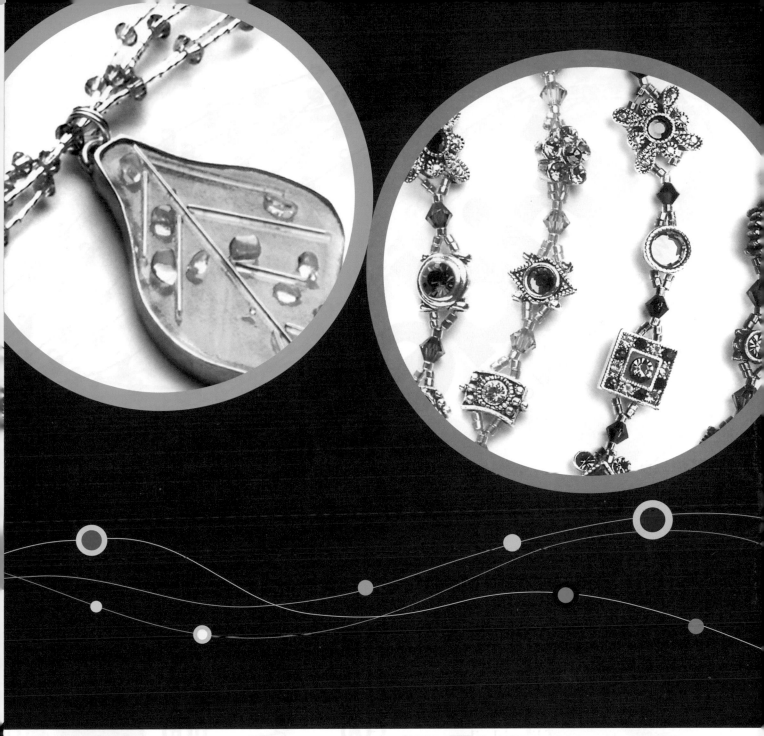

Crystals

Bloss

by Tracy Bretl

What began as a friend's request became this elegant set. It represents two of my favorite activities—designing with crystals and designing for the color and neckline of a specific dress. The floral fabric inspired the crystals and Delicas I chose, while the open-back dress sparked the addition of my favorite detail—the delicately trailing crystal dangles. By clustering the larger crystals I created the feel of flowers and ended up with a necklace that's as fresh as a summer bouquet.

oming
bouquet

Clusters of crystals converge in a sparkling set

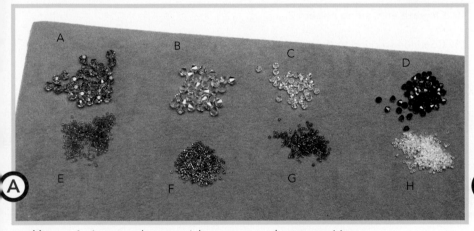

A

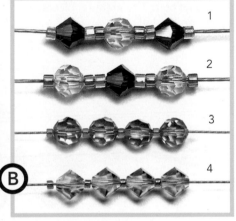

B

necklace • **1.** Arrange the materials on your workspace, pairing:
• 6mm round crystals (A) with Delicas matching the 6mm bicones (E);
• 6mm bicones (B) with Delicas matching the 6mm round crystals (F);
• 4mm round crystals (C) with Delicas matching the 4mm bicones (G); and
• 4mm bicone crystals (D) with Delicas matching the 4mm round crystals (H).

2. There are four patterns in this necklace (shown above):
Pattern 1: (H, D, H), (G, C, G), (H, D, H),
Pattern 2: (G, C, G), (H, D, H), (G, C, G),
Bicone flower (3): Delica E and crystal A alternated four times, and
Round flower (4): Delica F and crystal B alternated four times.

C

D

E

3. Determine the finished length of your necklace (mine is 15½ in./39cm). Add 25 in. (64cm) and cut a piece of .014 or .015 beading wire to that length.

4. String the round flower pattern and center the beads on the wire.

5. Pass the end of the wire back through the first three beads strung, and gently pull to create a flower.

6. To the right of the center flower, string pattern 1.

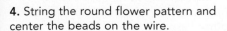

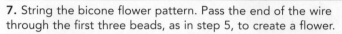

7. String the bicone flower pattern. Pass the end of the wire through the first three beads, as in step 5, to create a flower.

8. To the left of the center flower, string pattern 1.

9. Repeat step 7 to create a bicone flower on the left.

10. On each end, string pattern 2.

11. Continue working to the right and left of the center, alternating round and bicone flowers and alternating patterns 1 and 2, until the necklace is about 1 in. (2.5cm) from the desired length.

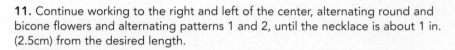

12. String a crimp bead, Delica, and the bottom loop of half the clasp. Go back through the Delica, crimp bead, and another Delica. Repeat on the other end. Tighten the wire, check the fit, and adjust if necessary. Crimp the crimp bead (Basic Techniques, p. 10).

13. To make the dangles, cut a 13-in. (33cm) and a 10-in. (25cm) piece of .010 beading wire.

14. Center Delica E on the 13-in. wire. Over both strands, string crystal A, Delica E, Delica F, crystal B, Delica F, Delica G, crystal C, Delica G, Delica H, crystal D, and Delica H. Repeat three times, beginning with Delica E.

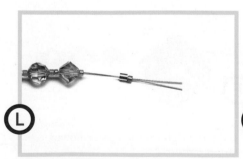

15. String Delica E, crystal A, Delica E, Delica F, crystal B, and Delica F. String a crimp bead and Delica F.

16. String both wires through the upper clasp loop and back through the Delica, crimp bead, and Delica. Tighten the wires, crimp the crimp bead, and trim the excess wire.

17. On the 10-in. wire, repeat step 14, but only repeat the pattern twice. String a crimp bead and Delica H. Repeat step 16 to finish the necklace, using the upper loop on the other clasp half.

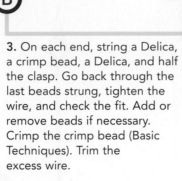

bracelet • 1. Determine the finished length of your bracelet, add 5 in. (13cm), and cut a piece of beading wire to that length.

2. The bracelet has two patterns:
Pattern 1: (F, B, F), (E, A, E), (F, B, F) and
Pattern 2: (G, C, G), (H, D, H), (G, C, G).
    Alternate patterns 1 and 2 until the bracelet is the desired length.

3. On each end, string a Delica, a crimp bead, a Delica, and half the clasp. Go back through the last beads strung, tighten the wire, and check the fit. Add or remove beads if necessary. Crimp the crimp bead (Basic Techniques). Trim the excess wire.

Supply List

necklace
all Delicas are size 11º
- **40** 6mm bicone crystals and 2g matching Delicas
- **36** 6mm round crystals and 2g matching Delicas
- **31** 4mm bicone crystals and 2g matching Delicas
- **31** 4mm round crystals and 2g matching Delicas
- flexible beading wire, .014 or .015
- flexible beading wire, .010
- **4** crimp beads
- two-strand box clasp
- chainnose or crimping pliers
- diagonal wire cutters

bracelet
all Delicas are size 11º
- **8** 6mm bicone crystals and 1g matching Delicas,
- **4** 6mm round crystals and 1g matching Delicas
- **8** 4mm bicone crystals and 1g matching Delicas

- **4** 4mm round crystals and 1g matching Delicas
- flexible beading wire, .014 or .015
- **2** crimp beads
- clasp
- chainnose or crimping pliers
- diagonal wire cutters

earrings
all Delicas are size 11º
- **2** 6mm bicone crystals and 2 matching Delicas
- **2** 6mm round crystals and 2 matching Delicas
- **2** 4mm bicone crystals and 2 matching Delicas
- **2** 4mm round crystals and 2 matching Delicas
- **2** 1½- or 2-in. (3.8cm or 5cm) head pins
- pair of lever-back earring wires
- chainnose and roundnose pliers
- diagonal wire cutters

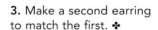

earrings • 1. String a head pin with crystal A, Delica F, crystal B, Delica G, crystal C, Delica H, crystal D, and Delica E.

2. Trim the head pin ⅜ in. (10mm) above the beads. Make a plain loop (Basic Techniques) above the top bead. Open the loop, slide on the earring wire, and close the loop.

3. Make a second earring to match the first. ❖

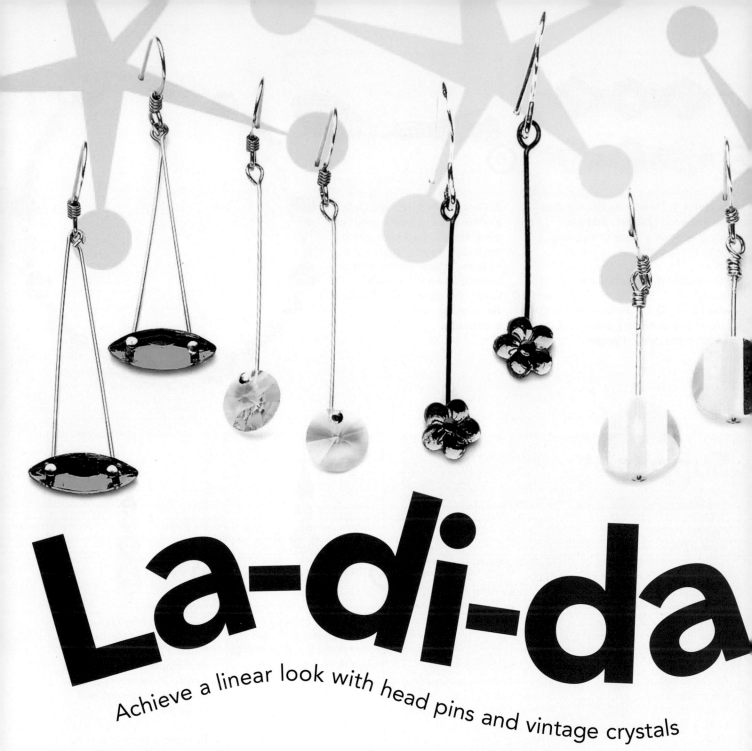

La-di-da

Achieve a linear look with head pins and vintage crystals

Dawdling always got me into trouble when I was a child. But as an adult, granting myself permission to drift results in some of my most creative designs. Such is the case with these earrings. When I gave myself time to dally over a pile of pretty crystals, my fascination with minimalist 1960s styles and the popularity of cascade earrings converged to form a series of fanciful earrings.

Supply List

- pair of vintage crystal sew-on components
- **2** 2½- or 3-in. (6.4 or 7.6cm) head pins
- pair of earring wires
- chainnose and roundnose pliers
- diagonal wire cutters

Kits are available for most of these earrings at BrendaSchweder.com.

by Brenda Schweder

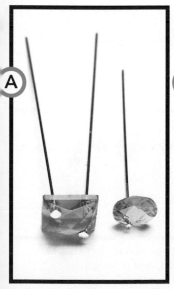

A

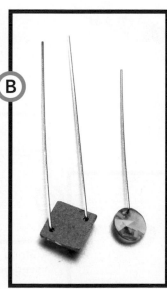

B

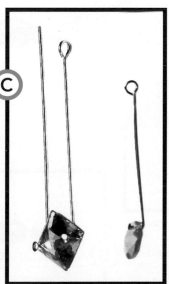

C

D

1. String a head pin through each hole in the crystal.

2. Bend the head pin against the back of the crystal to form a right angle.

3. Trim the head pin to the desired length. Make a plain loop (Basic Techniques, p. 10) at the end of each head pin.

4. Open an earring wire's loop and attach it to each earring's loop. Close the loop. Make a second earring to match the first. ❖

Ready,

Go from business to blue jeans with this pearl and crystal combo

Versatile jewelry keeps my fashion decisions and my life simple. Whether it's the soft blue-violet of cashmere or the faded blue of denim, this set can match any style. Crystals add sparkle, pearls bring sophistication, and the Czech glass beads provide shimmer—in sum, I have a set I can wear to work and straight to a date.

(A)

necklace • 1. Determine the finished length of your necklace (mine is 18½ in./47cm), add 6 in. (15cm), and cut a piece of beading wire to that length.

2. To make the dangles, string a glass bead, a seed bead, a bicone, and a seed bead on each of the five head pins. Make a plain loop above the top bead on each (Basic Techniques, p. 10).

(B)

3. Alternate seed beads with a glass bead, pearl, glass bead, and crystal. Repeat this pattern for 6 inches.

(C)

4. String a seed bead, a glass bead, a seed bead, and a dangle.

set, go!

by Kathy Siegel

D

E

5. Alternate the patterns in steps 3 and 4 until all five dangles are strung. Repeat the pattern in step 3 for 6 in. Check the fit, allowing for the length of the clasp, and add or remove beads evenly from each end as necessary.

6. String a crimp, a seed bead, and half the clasp. Go back through the last beads strung. Tighten the wire and crimp the crimp bead (Basic Techniques). Repeat on the other end of the necklace. Trim the excess wire.

SupplyList

both projects
- flexible beading wire, .014 or .015
- chainnose or crimping pliers
- diagonal wire cutters

necklace
- **66** 4mm fire-polished Czech glass beads, blue-violet
- **31** 4mm bicones, crystal
- **28** 5mm rice-shaped freshwater pearls, blue-violet
- hank of size 11º seed beads, blue-violet
- **5** 1-in. (2.5cm) head pins
- **2** crimp beads
- toggle clasp
- roundnose pliers

bracelet
- 4mm fire-polished Czech glass beads left over from necklace
- 4mm bicones left over from necklace
- 5mm rice-shaped freshwater pearls left over from necklace
- size 11º seed beads left over from necklace
- **2** crimp beads
- toggle clasp

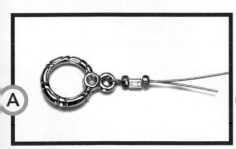

A

B

bracelet • 1. Determine the finished length, add 5 in. (13cm), and cut a piece of beading wire to that length.

2. String a seed bead, a crimp bead, a seed bead, and half the clasp. Go back through the last beads strung. Crimp the crimp bead.

3. Alternate seed beads with a glass bead, pearl, glass bead, and crystal. Repeat the pattern to within ½ in. (1.3cm) of the desired length, ending with a seed bead.

C

4. Finish the end of the bracelet as in step 6 of the necklace. ✤

Closely

These pieces are reminiscent of a 1940s slide bracelet that my mother-in-law gave me. To make a contemporary version, I started by selecting a variety of similar but not matched Swarovski crystal findings. Then I added crystal beads to unify the components. I've worked in a monochromatic palette, but don't feel limited to using only one color. Add a pair of shimmering earrings to complete the vintage look.

linked

by Anne Nikolai Kloss

Make a delicate bracelet and earrings with colorful Swarovski findings

(A)

(B)

(C)

bracelet • 1. Determine the finished length of your bracelet, add 5 in. (13cm), and cut two pieces of beading wire to that length. String a crystal, a crimp bead, and a round bead on both strands. String each strand through a loop on one of the clasp sections and back through the beads just strung. Tighten each wire and crimp the crimp bead (Basic Techniques, p. 10). Trim the excess wire.

2. Arrange your components before stringing, balancing assorted shapes, sizes, and colors.

String a Delica on both strands. Separate the strands and string two Delicas on each. Then string a charm on both wires. (Keep the wires from crossing or the charms will twist.) String two more Delicas on each strand, then string both strands through a Delica and a crystal.

Repeat the pattern six or more times, until the bracelet encircles your wrist.

3. String a crimp bead, a round bead, and the remaining clasp section. Make sure the clasp section is not upside down. Tighten the wires and crimp the crimp beads. Trim the excess wire.

Rhapsody in

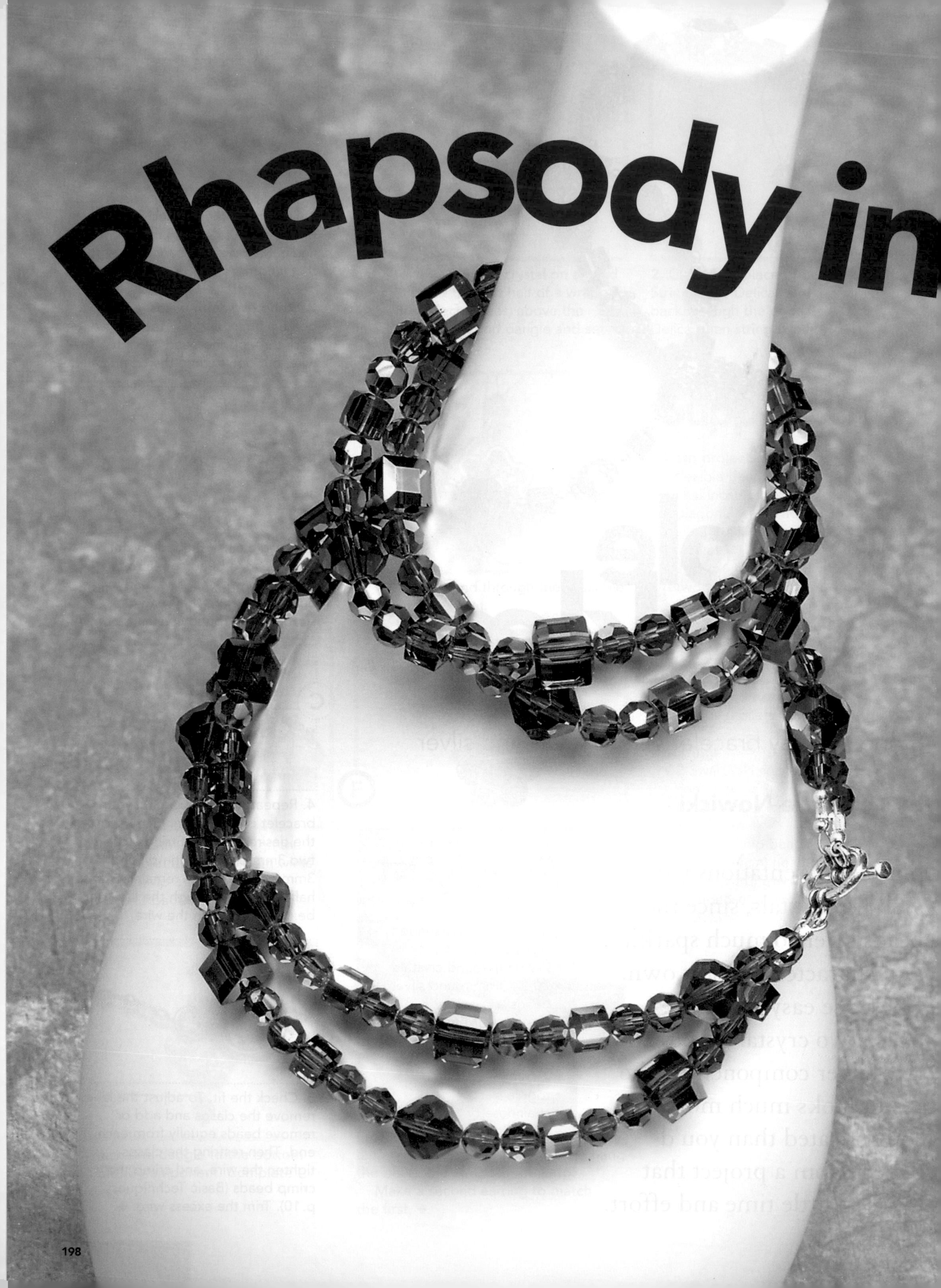

blue crystals

Compose a dazzling, double-strand necklace, bracelet, and earring set

by Lynne Dixon-Speller

I've never made a
piece of jewelry in my
birthstone color, so when
I spotted a strand of large
sparkling crystals with a
sapphire hue, I knew they'd
be going home with me.
I picked out nearly all the
shapes and sizes available
and ended up with so
many beads that instead
of making a single-strand
necklace as planned, I made
a double-strand version.
Of course, I also made a
matching bracelet and
earrings with the
leftover beads.

necklace • 1. Determine the finished length of your necklace's inner strand (mine is 17½./44cm) and add 6 in. (15cm). Cut one piece of beading wire to that length and one 1 in. (2.5cm) longer. On the longer strand, string a 6mm round crystal, 3mm bead, crimp bead, and 3mm. Go through the clasp's lower loop and back through the beads. Tighten the wire and crimp the crimp bead (Basic Techniques, p. 10). Trim the excess wire.

2. String a 10mm round crystal to begin the pattern shown. Repeat until the strand is the desired length. (The last repeat may not be a complete pattern.)

3. String a 3mm bead, a crimp bead, and a 3mm bead and go through the lower loop of the remaining clasp section. Go back through the last three beads, tighten the wire, and crimp the crimp bead. Trim the excess wire.

Crystal hue persuasion

Combine a spectrum of colors for a sparkling necklace and bracelet

by Diane Vickery

I enjoy making jewelry with my friend, Kathy, while we catch up on each other's lives. While looking over our latest purchases, several of the crystals caught my eye. I like the clear, vivid color and faceted brilliance of Swarovski crystals, and the rainbow of colors makes them a must-have. A bracelet is a great way to experiment with a gradation of colors—from the deep tones of blue zircon to the softness of peridot. I especially like the contrast of the touch of pink.

necklace • In steps 2–7, alternate the crystals with seed beads, as shown in the photos.

1. Determine the desired length of your necklace (mine measures 17½ in./45cm). Add 6 in. (15cm) and cut a piece of beading wire to that length.

2. Center the 8mm rose cube on the beading wire. Add a 6mm rose cube to each side.

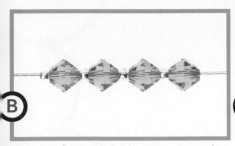

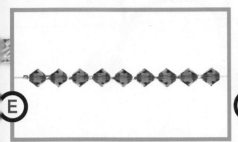

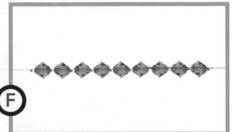

(B)

(C)

(D)

3. String four peridot bicones on each end of the necklace.

4. String eight aquamarine bicones on each end.

5. String two light sapphire bicones on each end.

(E)

(F)

6. String nine sapphire bicones on each end.

7. String nine blue zircon bicones on each end; finish with a seed bead. Tape one end of the necklace.

(G)

(H)

8. String two seed beads, a crimp bead, a seed bead, and the toggle on the untaped end. Go back through the seed bead, the crimp bead, and several adjacent beads on the strand. Tighten the beading wire until you have a small loop around the clasp. Crimp the crimp bead (Basic Techniques, p. 10). Trim the excess wire.

9. Remove the tape from the opposite end. String a seed bead, a crimp bead, a seed bead, and the clasp loop. Go back through the beads just strung and through several adjacent beads. Tighten the beading wire, so no excess wire shows between beads and the piece is flexible, not taut. Crimp the crimp bead. Trim the excess wire.

bracelet • *Alternate crystals with seed beads as in the necklace.*
1. Determine the desired finished length of your bracelet (mine measures 7¾ in./20cm). Add 5 in. (13cm) and cut a piece of beading wire to that length.

2. Center the 8mm rose bicone on the beading wire. String two peridot, four aquamarine, one light sapphire, five sapphire, and five blue zircon crystals on each side of the center pink bicone. Check the length and add or remove beads as necessary.

3. Finish as in steps 8 and 9 of the necklace, stringing wire through several beads beyond the crimp beads. ❖

Supply List

both pieces
- flexible beading wire, .014 or .015
- chainnose or crimping pliers
- diagonal wire cutters

necklace
- **18** 5mm bicone crystals, sapphire
- **18** 5mm bicone crystals, blue zircon
- **16** 5mm bicone crystals, aquamarine
- **8** 5mm bicone crystals, peridot
- **4** 5mm bicone crystals, light sapphire
- **2** 6mm cube-shaped crystals, light rose
- **1** 8mm cube-shaped crystal, light rose
- hank size 11º seed beads, silver-lined clear
- **2** crimp beads
- **1** toggle clasp

bracelet
- **10** 4mm bicone crystals, sapphire
- **10** 4mm bicone crystals, blue zircon
- **8** 4mm bicone crystals, aquamarine
- **4** 4mm bicone crystals, peridot
- **2** 4mm bicone crystals, light sapphire
- **1** 8mm bicone crystal, light rose
- size 11º seed beads, left over from necklace
- **2** crimp beads
- **1** toggle clasp

Trace of lace

Create a necklace with a delicate scallop design • by Anne Nikolai Kloss

Although I usually favor ethnic pieces made with heavier stones, the light and airy shape of this necklace intrigued me. I discovered the scallop technique accidentally. I wanted the design to emerge from a center focal bead in the necklace, but the wire kept arching. The shape was attractive, so I added dangles on each side. After establishing the design, I made several versions of this necklace, using crystal discs, hearts, and flowers for accent beads. I look for beads that will hang gracefully and are not too heavy. I also recommend that you store the necklace flat, so that it maintains its shape and doesn't kink.

Start this necklace at the middle of your wire to establish the symmetry of the piece. Don't vary from the wire's recommended size; the .014 or .015 provides resilience without stiffness.

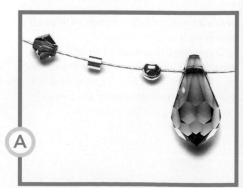

1. Cut a 34-in. (86cm) length of beading wire. To make the first dangle, string a 4mm bead, a crimp bead, a 3mm round bead, and an accent bead to the center of the wire.

SupplyList

- **5** accent beads for dangles
- **11-15** 4mm beads
- **5g** Delica beads
- **9** 3mm round silver beads
- flexible beading wire, .014 or .015
- **7** crimp beads
- lobster claw clasp
- soldered jump ring
- chainnose pliers or crimping tool
- diagonal wire cutters

2. Go back through the round bead, crimp bead, and 4mm bead. Tighten the wire, but allow enough space between the accent bead and the round bead so the drop hangs freely. Crimp the crimp bead (Basic Techniques, p. 10).

3. String 30 Delica beads on one end of the wire. Then, string a 4mm bead, a crimp bead, a round bead, and an accent bead, as before. Go back through the last three beads and crimp to make another dangle. Repeat on the other side of the center dangle.

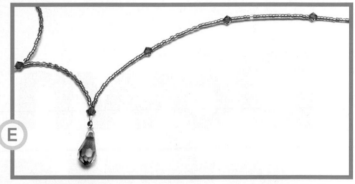

4. Repeat step 3 on each side of the necklace. Make a total of five dangles. String 25 Delicas on each side.

5. Determine the spacing for the 4mm beads. (For a 16-in. (41cm) necklace, string the 4mm beads at 25-seed bead intervals. For a longer necklace, increase the count to 30-seed bead intervals.

   String a pattern of one 4mm bead and 25 (or more) Delicas twice on each side. Add a 4mm bead and a few Delicas as needed to reach the desired length. For a 16-in. necklace, the necklace sides should extend approximately 4½ in. (11cm) beyond the last dangle on each side.

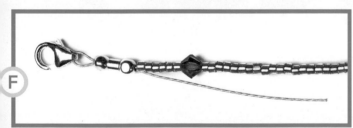

6. On one end, string a round bead, a crimp bead, another round, and the clasp. Go back through the last three beads strung. Tighten the wire until you have a small loop around the clasp. Crimp the crimp bead and trim the excess wire.

   To finish the other end, string a round bead, a crimp bead, another round, and a soldered jump ring. Go back through the last three beads strung. Tighten the wire, crimp the crimp bead, and trim the excess wire. ❖

Down the stretch

String a triple-strand elastic bracelet

by Lea Rose Nowicki

Wanting a variation on simple, single-strand bracelets, I came up with a three-strand stretch version. The core of this bracelet is a continuous piece of elastic. After you string the bracelet's first round to the desired size, repeat the pattern two more times. You can wear several of these bracelets together or make just one using two or three different colors of Czech fire-polished beads.

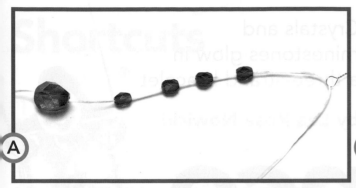

1. Cut a 30-in. (76cm) piece of ribbon elastic. Thread it through the twisted wire needle, keeping the tail fairly short. Put a piece of tape on the floss 4 in. (10cm) from the long end. String one 6mm bead and four 4mm beads.

2. For a 6½-in. (16.5cm) bracelet, repeat this pattern six more times. Measure the bracelet around your wrist. To make a longer bracelet, add one or more repeats. Go through the first 6mm bead again to close the circle. Pull the floss gently to eliminate any slack between the beads.

SupplyList

- **84** or more 4mm Czech fire-polished beads
- **7** or more 6-8mm Czech fire-polished beads
- Gossamer Floss or ribbon elastic
- twisted wire beading needles, medium
- G-S Hypo Cement
- scissors

3. String four 4mm beads (C) and go through the next 6mm bead again (D). Repeat six times, stopping before you go through the 6mm bead where you started. (You will end with four 4mm beads.)

4. Go through the first 6mm bead again and repeat step 3. You'll have gone through each 6mm bead three times.

5. Remove the tape and tie a surgeon's knot with the ends of the floss (Basic Techniques, p. 10).

6. Put a drop of glue on the knot. Trim the ends to ⅛ in. (3mm). Gently stretch the bracelet to pull the knot into the adjacent 6mm bead. ✤

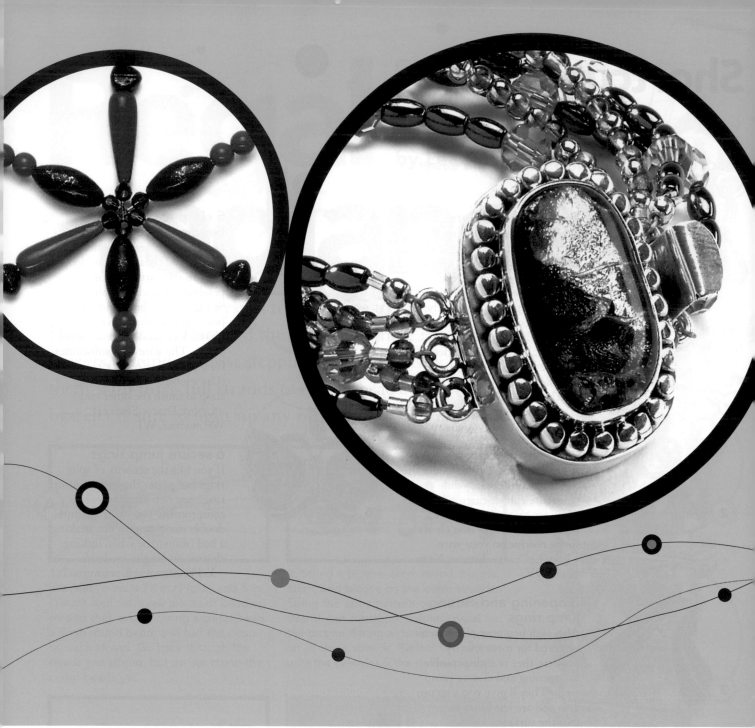

Mixed

media

Face it

Profile a whimsical face
bead on a seed bead and
pearl necklace

by Nancy Kugel

The friendly faces of artist Melanie Brooks' porcelain fairies motivated me to design this fun yet stylish necklace. I chose a monochromatic color scheme to give the piece a subtle quality, but if it's liveliness you want, go with contrasting hues. Whichever color scheme you choose, you'll not only finish this necklace within a couple of hours, but you'll be wearing a friendly face no matter what your mood.

Tip: Use chainnose pliers to make flat crimps. They're less likely to break small Delicas.

SupplyList

- fairy face pendant set (Melanie Brooks, PO Box 20002, Ferndale, MI 48220 or Earthenwood@ yahoo.com)
- 16-in. (41cm) strand Swarovski pearls
- 5g size 8º seed beads
- 5g size 11º Delica beads, matte
- 5g size 11º Delica beads, silver- or gold-lined
- 2 porcelain oval bead components (Melanie Brooks)
- 6 2-in. (51cm) head pins
- 3-in. (7.6cm) eye pin
- pendant bail (hanging loop)
- flexible beading wire, .012
- 8 crimp beads
- toggle clasp
- chainnose and roundnose pliers
- diagonal wire cutters

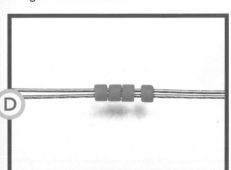

1. String a pearl and a size 8º seed bead onto a head pin. Turn a plain loop (Basic Techniques, p. 10) above the top bead. Make a total of six pearl dangles and set aside.

2. Remove the leaf and silver accent bead from the face pendant. Open the loop of an eye pin and attach the leaf and silver accent bead. Close the loop.

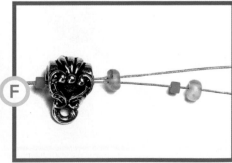

3. Remove the face, spacer, and crystal from the pendant and string them on the eye pin. Make the first half of a wrapped loop (Basic Techniques) above the top bead and set aside.

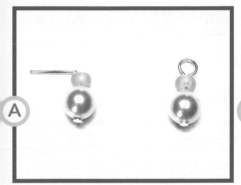

4. Cut two 14-in. (36cm) and two 10-in. (25cm) lengths of beading wire (the necklace measures 18 in./46cm). For a longer or shorter necklace, adjust the measurement of the 10-in. lengths of beading wire. Set aside the two 10-in. pieces. Center four matte Delicas over both 14-in. strands.

5. Center the bail over the Delicas and string an 8º on each side of the bail.

6. Separate the strands and string a matte Delica and an 8º on the lower strand.

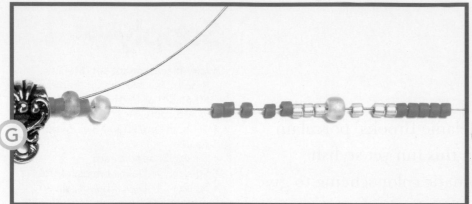

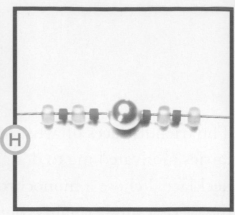

7. String a Delica pattern of five mattes, three silver-lined, an 8º seed bead, three silver-lined, and five mattes.

8. String a pearl pattern as shown. Alternate two 8ºs and two mattes on each side of a pearl.

String a Delica pattern, pearl pattern, and Delica pattern.

9. String an 8º, a matte, an 8º, a matte, a crimp bead, a matte, and the oval bead component. Go back through the last three beads, but do not crimp the crimp bead.

Repeat steps 6 through 9 on the other side of the bail to complete the lower strand.

10. On the upper strand string a matte and an 8º. String a Delica pattern and pearl pattern. Repeat. Repeat on the other side of the bail to complete the upper strand.

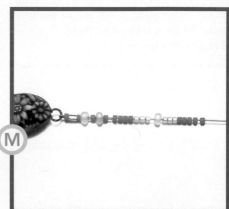

11. String a matte, a crimp bead, and a matte. Pass the wire through the oval bead's loop and go back through the last three beads. Do not crimp the crimp bead. Repeat on other end of the wire.

Tighten both wires, crimp the crimp beads (Basic Techniques), and trim the excess wire.

12. String a crimp bead and a matte on a 10-in. piece of beading wire. Pass the wire through the remaining loop of the oval bead and back through the last beads strung. Crimp the crimp bead.

13. String a matte, an 8º, a matte, and an 8º. Trim the excess wire. Alternate the Delica pattern and the pearl pattern until 3 in. (7.6cm) from the end. Tape the end. Repeat steps 12 and 13 on the other end of the necklace.

14. String a matte, a crimp bead, a matte, and half the toggle clasp. Go back through these beads and tighten the wire. Do not crimp the crimp beads. Repeat on the other end of necklace with the remaining clasp half. Check the fit and add or remove an equal number of beads on each end if necessary.

15. Open the loop on one of the pearl dangles. Attach it to the oval bead's loop between the lower strand and the bead. Close the loop.

Attach the two remaining pearl dangles to the loop as shown. Repeat on the other oval bead.

16. Slide the loop of the face dangle through the bail's loop and complete the wraps. ❖

Kits for this necklace are available at Nancy's website, engee-kay.com.

Embellish a suede bracelet with your favorite gemstones

Wrap star

by Naomi Fujimoto

Here's a way to use a handful of pretty gems without expending much energy designing: artfully display mini collections on a length of suede cord. Wrap it around your wrist three or four times, and that skinny suede becomes a chunky bracelet.

Supply List

- **20** or more assorted gemstones, pearls, crystals, and spacers
- **3 ft.** (91cm) or more suede lacing
- 26-gauge silver wire
- chainnose pliers
- diagonal wire cutters
- scissors

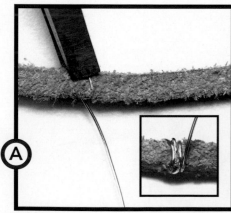

1. Cut a 12-in. (30cm) piece of wire. Use chainnose pliers to squeeze the end of the wire into the suede, 7 in. (18cm) from one end. Wrap the wire snugly two or three times around the suede.

2. Arrange groups of three to five beads and spacers. Each group will form a section of the bracelet. String a bead and wrap the wire snugly as before. String additional beads as desired, wrapping the wire between each bead.

3. To finish a beaded section, wrap the wire snugly around the suede two or three times. Trim the excess wire. Slide the end of the wire under one of the wraps and squeeze the wraps gently with pliers.

4. Wrap the suede around your wrist several times as desired. On each wrap, mark a small dot in the center of your wrist.

5. Wire beads to the suede as before, using the dots to center each beaded section. Before finishing each section, wrap the suede around your wrist to check the placement of the beads. Add or remove beads as necessary.

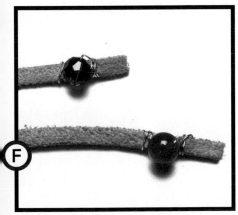

6. When you have beaded each section, wrap the suede around your wrist and tie the ends into a square knot. Trim each end of the cord 2½ in. (6.4cm) from the knot. (My bracelets are 32 in./81cm with four wraps.)

If desired, attach a bead near each end of the cord. ❖

Cool jewels

Spacers unite an assortment of beads in a playful bracelet • **by Beth Stone**

I've been told that I have an eye for putting together interesting and unusual color combinations. I let the beads speak to me, and my jewelry seems to design itself. To accumulate an assortment of beads to work with, I look for color and texture in my bead-hunting travels. In addition to pearls and gemstones, I often use vintage glass, which can be hard to find, as well as some good bead reproductions. When you work with a mix of beads, such as in the bracelets shown here, spacers play two roles: they add texture and unify diverse elements.

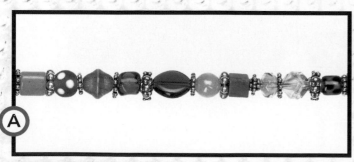

A

1. Determine the desired length of your bracelet. Add 5 in. (13cm) and cut a piece of beading wire to that length. String the beads and spacers in an alternating pattern, beginning and ending with a spacer.

B

2. String two seed beads or one 3mm bead, a crimp bead, another seed bead, and one half of the clasp. Go back through the beads just strung and a few adjacent beads. Tighten the beading wire until you have a small loop around the clasp. Crimp the crimp bead (Basic Techniques, p. 10) and trim the excess wire.

3. Repeat step 2 to attach the remaining clasp half. Keep the bracelet flexible, not taut, with no excess wire showing between the beads. ❖

SupplyList

- **16** or more assorted metal spacers
- **15** or more beads, 3-10mm, assorted shapes and colors
- toggle clasp
- flexible beading wire, .014 or .015
- **2** crimp beads
- **2** 3mm metal beads or **6** size 8° seed beads
- chainnose or crimping pliers
- diagonal wire cutters

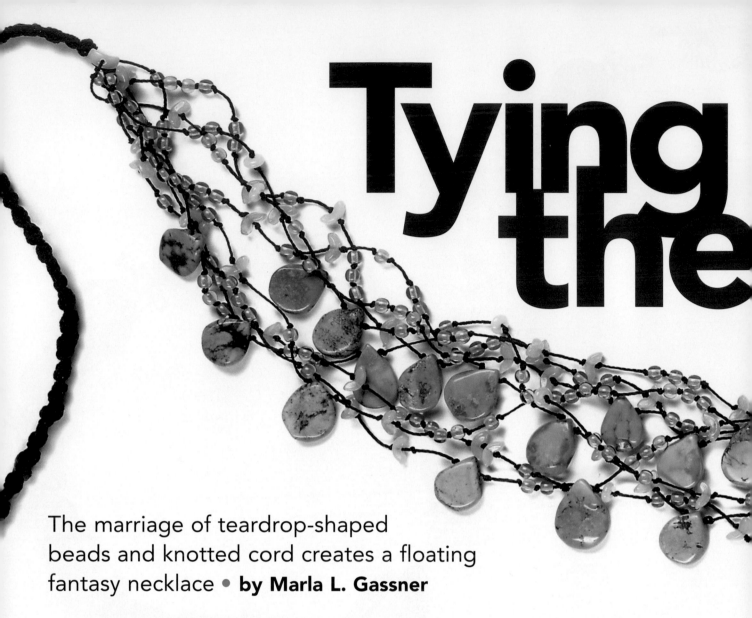

Tying the

The marriage of teardrop-shaped beads and knotted cord creates a floating fantasy necklace • **by Marla L. Gassner**

I receive many requests to teach classes on my floating fantasy necklace. The instructions first appeared in my 1997 book, *The Bead and I*. For the novice beader, the instructions have been simplified by using fewer strands and substituting overhand knots for the macramé on the ends. I recommend that you cut a length of waxed cord and practice making overhand knots before you attempt a necklace—you'll soon learn how to land knots exactly where you want them. Although an awl is optional, I find it invaluable for moving and manipulating knots.

The eight-strand turquoise necklace measures 37 in. (94cm); the five-strand jasper necklace, 32 in. (81cm).

1. Cut 8 ft. (2.4m) of cord for each of the strands you're making. Put a drop of Fray Check on each end.

Tie an overhand knot (Basic Techniques, p. 10) approximately 2 ft. (61cm) from the end of one strand.

knot

2. String a 4mm bead or rondelle against the knot. Make a loose overhand knot next to the bead. Use an awl or your fingers to slide the knot into position. Tighten the knot. (To undo a knot, insert the awl into it and slide it away.)

3. String individual beads and groups of two or three beads, tying a knot before and after each bead. Leave approximately ¼ -½ in. (6mm-1cm) of space between some beads and bead groups, as shown. Add four or five teardrop-shaped beads at approximately equal intervals or vary their placement as desired. Make the beaded section of the strand 16-19 in. (41-48cm) long, depending on the finished length of your necklace. End the strand with a 4mm round or spacer bead.

A

B

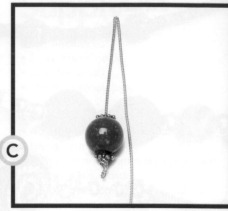

C

Tracy Bay's hook-and-eye clasp •
1. Cut two 5-in. (13cm) lengths of twisted wire.

2. Make a wrapped loop (Basic Techniques, p. 10) at one end of a wire and string on a round bead. Add spacers, if desired. Make a larger wrapped loop above the bead.

3. Use roundnose pliers to shape any remaining wire into a decorative swirl. Flatten the decoration against the bead.

4. Make a wrapped loop at the end of the second piece of wire. String a round bead above the loop, adding spacers as desired. Fold the wire 1 in. (2.5cm) above the bead. Squeeze the wire together with chainnose pliers.

SupplyList

Tracy Bay's hook-and-eye clasp
• 10 in. (25cm) 20- or 22-gauge twisted wire
• **2** 10-12mm round beads
• **4** spacers (optional)
• chainnose and roundnose pliers
• diagonal wire cutters

button-and-loop clasp
• 1g seed beads
• 8-10mm bead or button
• large-hole spacer (optional), 2mm
• **2** crimp beads
• chainnose pliers
• diagonal wire cutters

S-hook clasp
• 2 in. (5cm) 20- or 22-gauge wire
• spacer bead (optional)
• **2** split rings or soldered jump rings
• ball-peen hammer
• bench block or anvil
• roundnose pliers
• diagonal wire cutters

D

E

5. Place your roundnose pliers about ½ in. (1.3cm) above the bead and bend the doubled wire toward you. Gently shape the tip into a hook.

6. Wrap the end around both wires. Form a decorative swirl, as in step 3, with the end. Trim the excess.

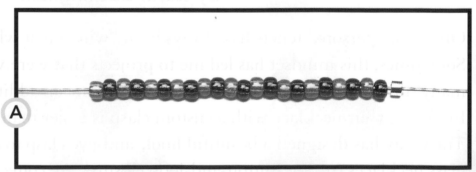

A

button-and-loop clasp • 1. Add an additional 4 in. (10cm) to the wire measurement of your bracelet or necklace. String a crimp bead and approximately 1 in. of seed beads on the end.

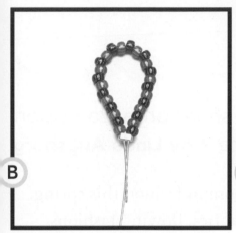

B

C

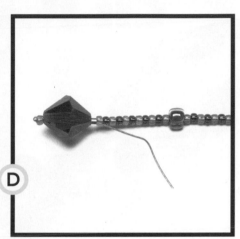

D

2. Go back through the crimp bead. Check the size of the loop to be sure it fits snugly over the bead or button. Crimp the crimp bead (Basic Techniques).

3. To hide the crimp bead, make a folded crimp (Basic Techniques) in step 2 and slide a large-hole (2mm) bead over the crimp.

4. String your necklace or bracelet.

5. String a crimp bead, an 8-10mm bead or button, and a seed bead at the end. Go back through the large bead and the crimp bead. Tighten the wire and crimp the crimp bead. Trim the excess wire.

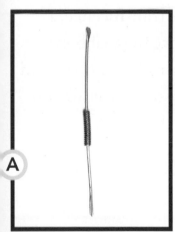

A

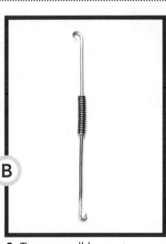

B

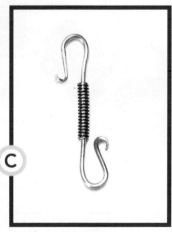

C

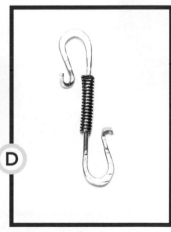

D

Practice this technique with inexpensive copper wire before attempting it with higher-quality wire.

S-hook clasp • 1. Cut a 2-in. (5.1cm) length of wire. If desired, slide a spacer bead on the wire for decoration. Hammer the tips of the wire.

2. Turn a small loop at each end.

3. About ¼ to ½ in. (6 to 13 mm) from one end, grasp the wire with the lower section of your roundnose pliers and shape one half of the S curve. At the same distance from the other end, bend a curve in the opposite direction.

4. Hammer the curves to strengthen the wire. Finish your necklace with a split ring or soldered jump ring at each end. Use the clasp to fasten the necklace. The clasp can be fastened or unfastened from either side. ✣

Gossamer and glass

Art beads grace sheer organza ribbon in a delicate necklace • **by Linda Augsburg**

Romance is abloom in fashion this spring. Diaphanous fabrics, flowing fashions, and all things soft are in style. These handmade glass beads from Nancy Tobey capture that look with their swirls of color encased in glass. To accentuate their translucence, I strung them on organza ribbons. Braiding the sheer ribbons, bedecked with accent beads, adds substance without compromising the airiness of the piece.

Use true ¼-in. organza ribbon and beads with 1mm holes; the beads stay in place but the ribbon can be inserted without much effort. Some ribbon marked ¼ in. is actually wider and makes stringing more difficult.

blue necklace • 1. Stack three or four 2-ft. (61cm) lengths of ribbon. Cut a 5-in. (13cm) piece of beading wire. Fold the ends of the ribbons over the center of the wire and fold the wire in half. Using the wire as a needle, string and center the art beads over all the ribbons.

2. Separate the ribbons. Use the wire as before on individual ribbons and slide on accent beads. Weave or braid the ribbons. Adjust the bead placement as desired.

3. Determine the finished length of the necklace (mine is 17 in./4c3m with a 2½-in./6.4cm chain extender). Stack the ribbon ends and fold each stack at that length, considering the length of the clasp and keeping the focal bead centered. Place one fold into a pinch clasp. Use chainnose pliers to close the clasp. Make sure the ribbons are secure. Trim the ribbon ends along the edge of the clasp. Repeat on the other end.

4. Slide an accent bead onto a head pin and make the first half of a wrapped loop (Basic Techniques, p. 10). Slide the end link of the chain into the loop and complete the wraps.

5. Use a jump ring to attach the other end of the chain to the loop of one pinch clasp (Basic Techniques).

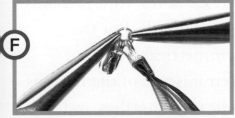

6. Repeat step 5 to attach the lobster claw clasp to the other pinch clasp.

Supply List

- art beads, set of **5** or **1** focal and **2** coordinating (Nancy Tobey, 978-772-3317, nancytobey.com)
- 2 ft. (61cm) each of ¼-in. (6mm) organza ribbon, three or four colors
- **30-40** assorted accent beads or crystals, 6-9mm
- 2½-in. (6.3cm) open-link chain
- 2-in. (5.1cm) head pin
- flexible beading wire, .010
- **2** 8mm pinch clasps (Rio Grande, 800-545-6566, riogrande.com)
- lobster claw clasp
- **2** 4mm jump rings
- chainnose and roundnose pliers
- diagonal wire cutters
- scissors

pink necklace • 1. Repeat step 1 of the blue necklace, using one focal bead in the center.

2. Repeat step 2 of the blue necklace, stringing a few beads on each ribbon. Braid the ribbons. String a coordinating art bead over all the ribbons. Continue to string and braid beyond the art beads.

3. Follow steps 3 through 6 of the blue necklace to finish the necklace. ✤

Pretty in pink, peach, and plum, the intense colors of Lucite look best when strung simply, yet a simple piece can still be bold in its arrangement. Look for vintage beads at thrift stores or flea markets and mix them with contemporary beads. For the necklace, I chose clear and opaque beads to surround an asymmetrical cluster of flowers. The bracelet contains different sizes of teardrops, reminiscent of the buttons on an old cardigan. To complete the ensemble, I dangled delicate butterflies and crystals in earrings with varying lengths of chain.

Lucite flowers and butterflies enhance a necklace, bracelet, and earring trio

by Naomi Fujimoto

Garden party

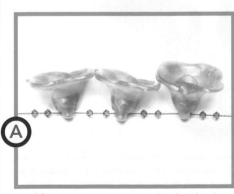

A

B

C

necklace • 1. Determine the finished length of your necklace (mine is 15 in./ 38cm), add 6 in. (15cm), and cut a piece of beading wire to that length. String two crystals and a flower. Repeat twice, then string two crystals.

2. On each side of the flowers, string an oval, crystal, rondelle, crystal, carved round, crystal, rondelle, crystal, round, crystal, rondelle, and crystal.

On one end, repeat the pattern, then string an oval and a crystal. On the other end, string an oval, crystal, rondelle, and crystal. Check the fit, adding or removing beads as necessary. The flowers will lie slightly off-center.

3. String a 3mm spacer, crimp bead, spacer, and the clasp. Go back through the last beads strung, tighten the wire, and crimp the crimp bead (Basic Techniques, p. 10). Repeat on the other end, using a soldered jump ring in place of the clasp.

String a hollow
glass bead on suede
lacing for a simple
and stylish necklace

Touch
of glass

by Rupa Balachandar

This understated design epitomizes summertime, when simple styles rule. A soft shade of suede encircles your neck, while basic knotting techniques keep sparkling rhinestone rondelles in place. Add a flat, subtly patterned, blown glass bead as a centerpiece and you're ready for some summer fun.

Supply List

- 20-25mm flat blown glass bead
- **12** 6mm rhinestone rondelles
- 3 ft. (91cm) ¼-in. (6.3mm) soft suede lacing
- scissors

1. Cut two 18-in. (46cm) lengths of suede lacing. Cut one end of each into a thin point.

2. Make an overhand knot (Basic Techniques, p. 10) 8 in. (20cm) from the pointed end of each piece.

3. Working from the pointed end, string three rondelles on each piece, flush with the knot.

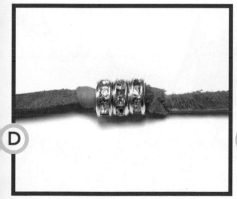

4. Tie an overhand knot on each piece next to the third rondelle.

5. Tie the lacing pieces together 1¼ in. (3.2cm) from the last overhand knots. String the glass bead over both pieces. Tie the lacing pieces together below the glass bead.

6. String three rondelles on one piece of lacing, placing them 1 in. (2.5cm) from the last knot. Tie an overhand knot just below the rondelles and trim the lacing to the length desired. Repeat on the other piece, placing the rondelles 2 in. (5.1cm) from the last knot.

7. Tie overhand knots ⅜ in. (1cm) from the ends at the back of the necklace. To wear, knot the lacing pieces together at the length desired. ❖

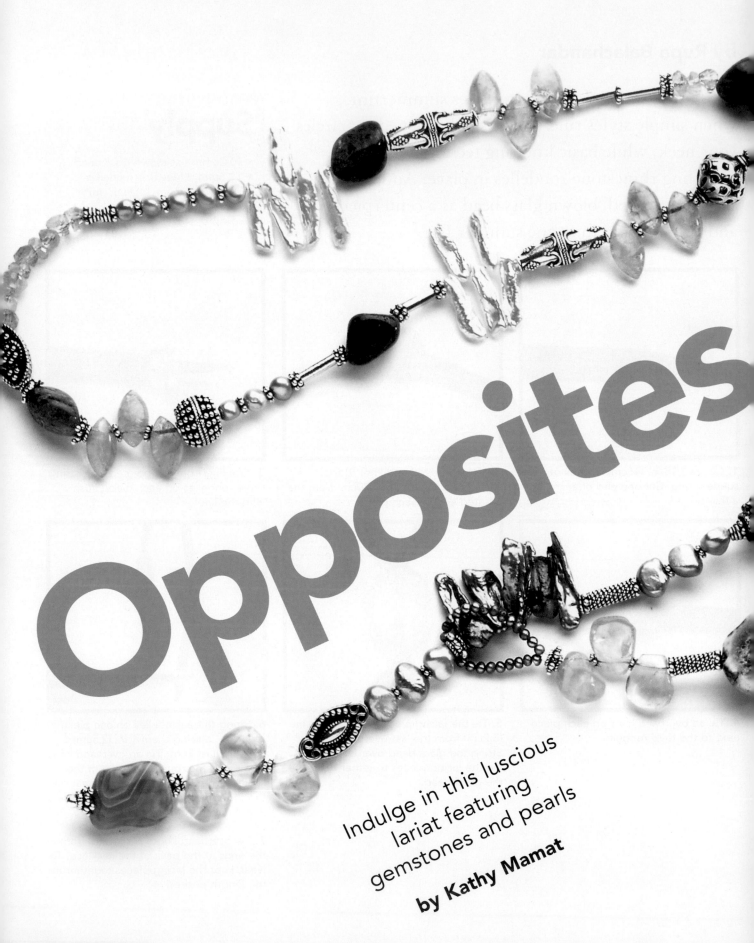

Opposites

Indulge in this luscious lariat featuring gemstones and pearls

by Kathy Mamat

attract

Rough and smooth, long and short, rectangular and round—this necklace is a celebration of contrasts, a display of diversity, a parade of paradox. Its asymmetrical design allows room for creativity and flexibility in choosing materials. Stringing this lariat is the perfect way to use up partial strands left from other projects; there's plenty of room for an unmatched bead, a stray gemstone, or a lonely spacer to find a home. If you choose to start from scratch this necklace is a splurge, but one that's well worth it.

Ⓐ

1. Determine the finished length of your necklace (mine are 24 in./61cm, tail to loop), add 9 in. (23cm), and cut a piece of beading wire to that length.

2. String a 4mm round bead, a bead cap, and a crimp bead. Go back through the bead cap and the crimp bead and tighten the wire. Crimp the crimp bead (Basic Techniques, p. 10) inside the bead cap.

3. String a nugget and a bead cap. Begin stringing gemstones interspersed with spacers and larger beads. I used sets of three and five, and purposely kept the order random and the necklace asymmetrical. *Note: The first 3 in. (7.6cm) of the necklace will dangle through the loop of the lariat. After 3 in., string five stick pearls. The stick pearls will be the stopper for the loop.*

Continue stringing sets of pearls, gemstones, and silver until the necklace is about 1 in. (2.5cm) shorter than your desired length.

4. String a crimp bead and 2 in. (5.1cm) of seed beads. Go back through the crimp bead and then through the spacers. Make sure the dangle will fit through the loop. Adjust the loop's size by adding or removing seed beads, if necessary. Tighten the wire and check the fit; adjust if necessary. Crimp the crimp bead and trim the excess wire.

5. To wear the necklace, drape it around your neck and drop the straight end through the loop end. ✤

Supply List

- gemstone nuggets, approx. 18mm
- stick pearls, approx. 20 x 5mm
- top-drilled gemstone drops, approx. 8 x 12mm
- freshwater pearls in two colors, approx. 5mm
- gemstone chips, approx. 5mm
- bead caps
- oval accent beads, approx. 10 x 15mm
- tube-shaped accent beads, approx. 4 x 10mm
- round accent beads, approx. 15mm
- 4-5mm spacers or accent beads
- 4mm round bead
- 1g size 6º or 8º seed beads
- flexible beading wire, .014 or .015
- **2** crimp beads
- chainnose or crimping pliers
- diagonal wire cutters

Compliments

by Naomi Fujimoto

Brilliant crystals and gold spacers embrace an embroidered silk pendant

Dainty and ladylike, this Russian pendant features a bouquet of blue and pink flowers on a silk background. There are countless options for showcasing it—with creamy pearls, on bright gold chain, or along a strand of matching beads. My approach? Crystals in the colors of the embroidered flowers surround the pendant while chartreuse beads mimic their foliage. Whatever you decide, you'll get compliments on your compliments.

SupplyList

- 33mm round embroidered silk pendant
- **6** 6mm round crystals, colors to match the pendant
- 16-in. (.41m) strand 4mm Czech fire-polished beads
- 1g size 11º seed beads
- **52** or more 5mm flat spacers
- 6mm jump ring
- flexible beading wire, .014 or .015
- **2** crimp beads
- magnetic clasp
- **2** pairs of chainnose pliers
- diagonal wire cutters
- crimping pliers (optional)

1. Determine the finished length of your necklace (mine is 17 in./43cm), add 6 in. (15cm), and cut a piece of beading wire to that length. Open a jump ring (Basic Techniques, p. 10). String the pendant on the ring and close it. Center the pendant over three seed beads on the wire.

2. On each side of the pendant, string a 6mm round crystal, spacer, crystal, spacer, crystal, and spacer.

3. On each end, string four 4mm beads interspersed with seed beads, two spacers, four 4mm beads interspersed with seed beads, and five spacers. Repeat two or more times until the necklace is 1 in. (2.5cm) from the desired length.

4. String a crimp bead, seed bead, and half the clasp. Go back through these beads and a few additional beads and tighten the wire. Repeat on the other end. Check the fit; adjust if needed. Crimp the crimp beads (Basic Techniques) and trim the excess wire. ❖

Center stage

Art beads shine in a casual lariat

by Heather Powers

I created this lariat-style necklace to spotlight my art beads, and I love its carefree and flexible design. The asymmetrical beads play a leading role, while crystals and silver comprise the supporting cast. Make it long or short by adjusting the length of the seed bead rope, and you'll have a necklace that steals the show.

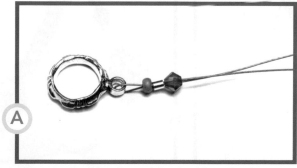

1. Determine the desired finished length of your necklace without the dangle (mine is 24 in./61cm). Add 6 in. (15cm) and cut a piece of beading wire to that length.

String a 4mm crystal, a crimp bead, a seed bead, and the loop end of the toggle on one end of the wire. Go back through the beads, tighten the wire, and make a folded crimp (Basic Techniques, p. 10). Trim the excess wire.

SupplyList

- **2** polymer clay art beads (Heather Powers, humblebeads.com)
- **3** 8mm round beads, turquoise
- **2** 6mm round beads, turquoise
- **6** 6mm bicone crystals, **3** each in two colors
- **6** 4mm bicone crystals, **3** each in two colors
- **6** 5mm freshwater pearls, **3** each in two colors
- **4** 8mm flat spacer beads
- **6** 4mm flat spacer beads
- 6g size 8º seed beads
- flexible beading wire, .014 or .015
- **4** crimp beads
- **4** 2mm round spacer beads
- toggle clasp
- chainnose and crimping pliers
- diagonal wire cutters

by Irina Miech

To maximize the wearability of a necklace, I like to work an interchangeable element into the design. Since this necklace easily converts from one strand to two, you get double the return for your stringing efforts.

I began with a striking art bead, and then chose a monochromatic palette of pearls and crystals to enhance its subtle undertones. Incorporating lighter shades of colors on the outer strand brought the colors to life. Either way it's worn—as a single-strand with a turtleneck or as a double-strand with a scoop neck—you'll enjoy the versatility of the design.

1. Determine the finished length of your necklace. (My top strand measures 17 in./43cm; the bottom strand is 2 in./5cm longer.) Add 6 in. (15cm) to each measurement and cut a piece of beading wire to each length.

2. Center a bicone, the art bead, and a bicone on the longer strand of beading wire.

3. String a 6mm pearl, a bicone, a 3mm pearl, and a bicone interspersed with seed beads. Repeat the pattern for approximately 8 in. (20cm) on each side of the art bead. Tape the ends.

4. On the shorter strand of beading wire, string a bicone, a 6mm pearl, a disc, a rondelle, and a disc interspersed with seed beads. Repeat the pattern to within 3 in. (8cm) of each end of the necklace. Tape the ends.

or duet

Convert a medley of
pearls and crystals into a
single- or double-strand necklace

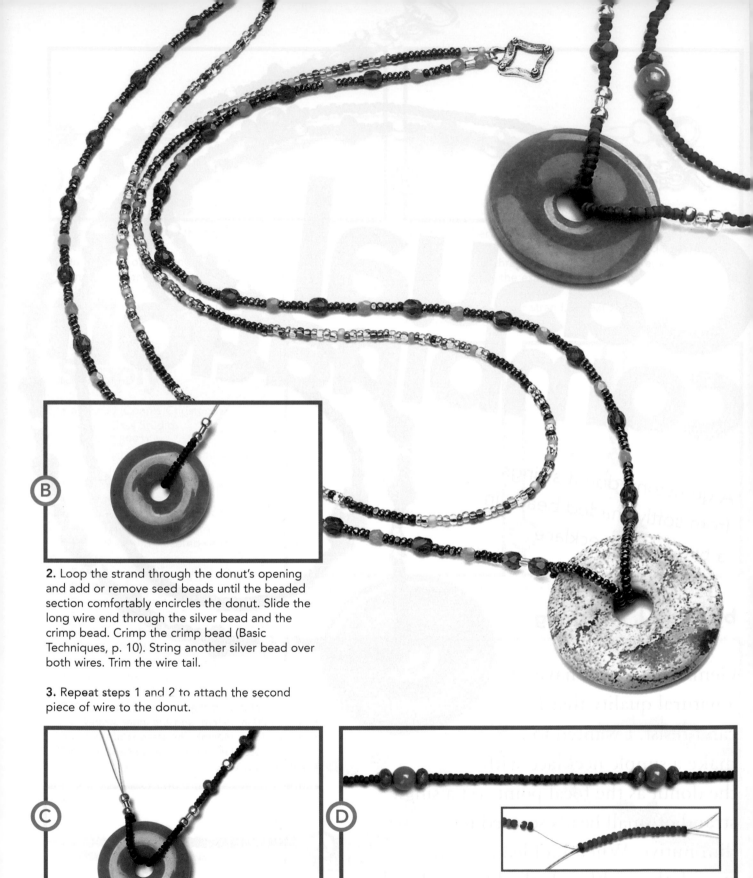

B

2. Loop the strand through the donut's opening and add or remove seed beads until the beaded section comfortably encircles the donut. Slide the long wire end through the silver bead and the crimp bead. Crimp the crimp bead (Basic Techniques, p. 10). String another silver bead over both wires. Trim the wire tail.

3. Repeat steps 1 and 2 to attach the second piece of wire to the donut.

C

4. On each strand, string a pattern of five blue seed beads, a faceted glass bead, five seed beads, and a silver bead until you are 8½ in. (22cm) from the donut. Tape each end.

D

5. Cut a 22-in. (56cm) length of beading wire. Center a 5mm bead on the strand. String a faceted bead on each side. String 2 in. (5cm) of seed beads, a faceted bead, a 5mm bead, and a faceted bead on each end until the strand measures 16 in. (41cm). To make stringing the seed beads easier, keep the beads on their original thread and simply slide them onto the wire. Tape each end.

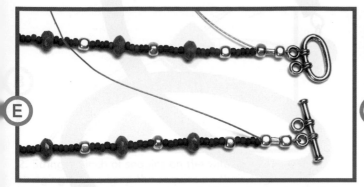

6. Remove the tape from one end of the donut strand. String a silver bead, a crimp bead, a silver bead, and the outer loop of the toggle bar. Go back through the beads just strung. Tighten the wire and crimp the crimp bead. Repeat on the opposite end with the toggle ring.

7. Repeat step 6 with the shorter strand, this time going through the inner loops on the toggle clasp.

brown and gold necklace • 1. Cut two 18-in. (46cm) lengths of beading wire. Repeat steps 1 and 2 of the blue and russet necklace, substituting 4mm beads for the silver beads.

2. On each strand, string a pattern of five seed beads, one 3mm bead, five seed beads, and a 4mm bead until you are 10 in. (25cm) from the donut. Tape each end.

3. Cut a 24-in. (61cm) length of beading wire. Tape one end. String 2 in. (5cm) of variegated seed beads and ½ in. (1.3cm) of brown seed beads onto the wire. (Refer to step 5 of the blue and russet necklace for an easy stringing tip.) Repeat until the beaded section measures 18 in. (46cm). Tape the other end.

4. Finish as in steps 6 and 7 of the blue and russet necklace, stringing 3mm beads or large seed beads in place of the silver beads and stringing both strands through the clasp loop. ✦

Retro

Beaded snowflakes are not a new ornament idea, so the perennial favorite required a fresh approach. "What can we try that's unconventional?" we asked. We found beads made of plastic, paper, and wood at thrift stores, then strung our vintage beads in unusual combinations of colors and shapes. Adding a few crystals creates a lively contrast to the other beads, making the look both retro and upscale.

If a form is bent, straighten it before stringing beads; bent spokes can cause crystals to break. Also, we recommend storing your ornaments in flat boxes.

1. To design a snowflake, create arrangements using beads of different colors, shapes, sizes, and finishes. On one spoke, string a 6mm or smaller bead to the center of the form. String assorted beads to the length desired, allowing at least ⅜ in. (1cm) to finish the end. (For smaller snowflakes, string only 2 in./5cm or so of beads.) Tape the end.

2. Repeat the same pattern on the remaining spokes or alternate patterns on adjacent spokes. Tape each end.

flakes

by Naomi Fujimoto

Snowflake ornaments give new life to old beads

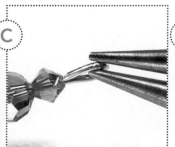

3. When you like the arrangement, remove the tape from one spoke and use roundnose pliers to turn a small loop. Repeat to finish the other spokes.

4. Cut a piece of ribbon approximately 7 in. (18cm) long. String it through one of the loops.

5. Bring the ends together and tie an overhand knot. Adorn a tree, window, or gift with the snowflake and enjoy the compliments on your handiwork. ❖

Supply List

- metal snowflake form
- assorted beads (crystals, vintage, seed beads)
- ribbon
- roundnose pliers
- scissors
- diagonal wire cutters